To Jane -
Happy Gardening
Nancy Goslee Power
XI-21-2009

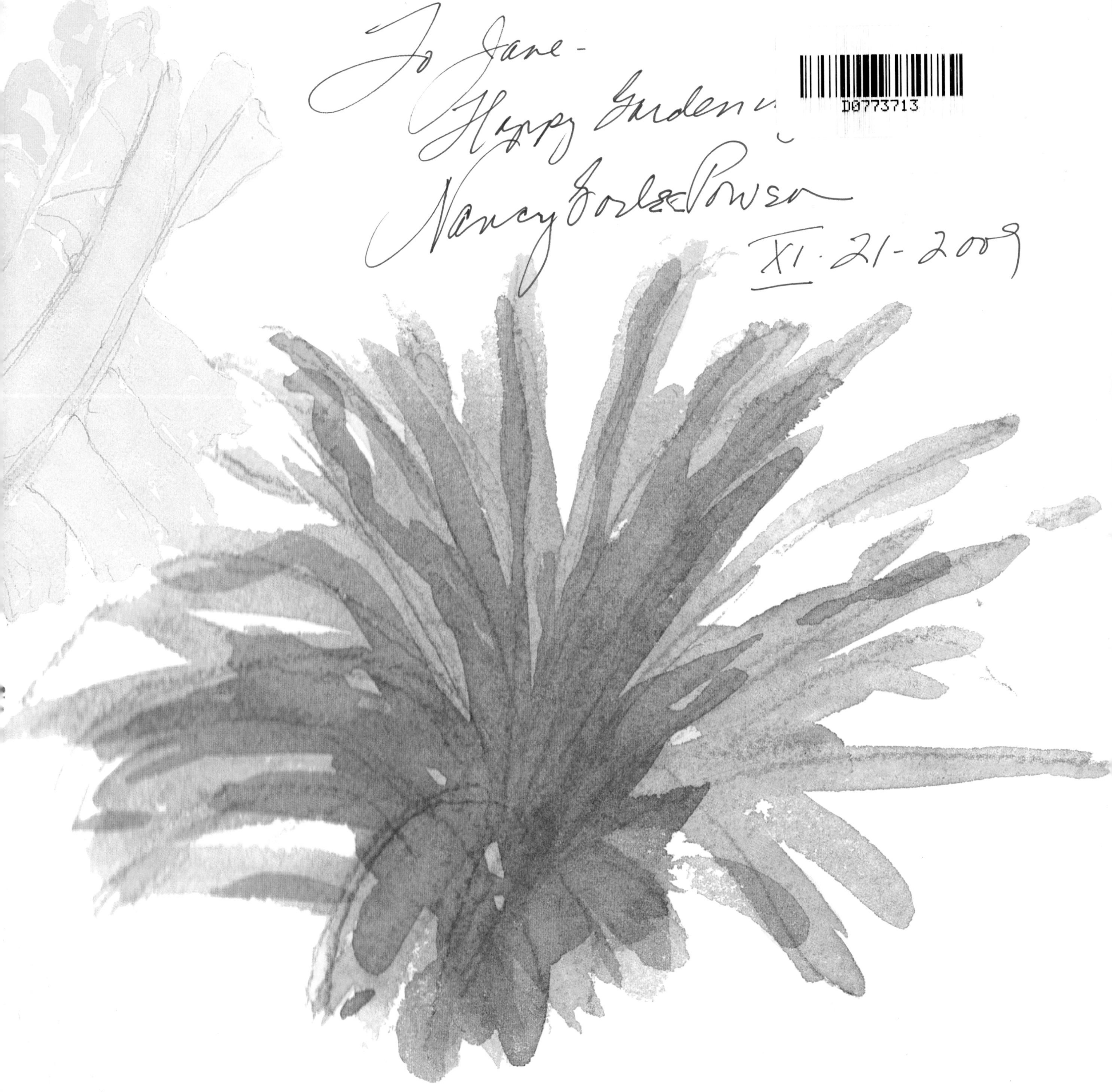

Power of Gardens

Power of Gardens

Nancy Goslee Power

FOREWORD BY BUNNY WILLIAMS

Stewart, Tabori & Chang, New York

Dedication

This book is dedicated to all of the talented designers who have worked in my studio and helped me design and create the gardens in this book. You've helped make my dreams come true.

Carolyn Doepke Bennett, Paul Blazek, Anne Marie Burke, Thomas B. Cox, Benjamin Claven, John Feldman, Howard Formby, Kathleen Frankle Null, Daniel Garness, Wade Graham, Ryan Gutierrez, Joanna Hankamer, William Hardman, Dryden Jenny Helgoe, John Henro, Daniel Hua, Julia Hubbard, Linda Jassim, Christian Kikklla, Serena Reed Kursusrow, Marcia Lee, Anya Lehman, Laurie B. Lewis, Joseph Marek, Dragan Mrdja, Dale Newman, William Nicholas, Victoria Pakshong, Sally Ann Paul, Jeff Pervorse, Barry Price, Elisa Read, Paul Robbins, Chris Sherwin, Douglas Stanton, Joe Sturges, Brian Tichenor, Donna West

Page 1: *Pole beans in the Moraga Vineyard's kitchen garden.*
Pages 2-3: *The Gardens at Live Oaks offer many different experiences.* Right: Agave attenuata, *my favorite plant.*

Contents

Foreword

First, there must be full disclosure. Nancy Power is one of my dearest friends. We met in New York when we were in our mid twenties. From the day we met, her warmth, humor, intelligence, and yes, her style have enriched my life. But what is so thrilling for me is to see how this dear person, with whom I speak every Sunday, has taken all these qualities and become a major force in the landscape design community.

As Nancy started her design career with interior design, it is natural that her gardens always begin from within a home. The relationship between the interior and exterior starts off her designs for the landscape, and her ability to create a harmonious flow of garden spaces or "rooms" is amazing.

Nancy is an artist and this really comes across as you study her gardens. Her amazing sense of color produces unexpected and exciting combinations. She is also a great plantswoman and her mixture of plant textures creates the most exciting sculptural combinations.

Nancy is both a traditionalist and a modernist. She has traveled the world looking at gardens from the sixteenth century in Italy to twentieth-century ones by Luis Barragan in Mexico and Roberto Burle Marx in Brazil. When I went to see the gardens at the Norton Simon Museum in Pasadena (one of my favorite museums) I was in awe of the amazing creation of my dear friend. The sculptures look so at home in this fabulous garden. Her other public gardens are always inviting and are oases of calm and beauty.

Along with her busy career she has found time to share her passion for designing gardens with children in inner city school programs. Nothing makes her happier than seeing the children rush to the garden to see their plants thriving in the California sun. I am so very proud of my friend.

—Bunny Williams

Spanish bluebells, iris, and primroses in the Doheny spring garden.

Introduction

Power of Gardens includes what I think are the best gardens my studio has designed and built over the last twenty-five years. What has motivated me to write this book is the desire to have a proper record of these gardens and to state my mission and purpose in my own voice. Most of all I want to share the images and the ideas behind the gardens with others who might be interested. This book is my contribution to the art of garden design in what has become known as the California Style: a relaxed, easy, inviting, and comfortable way of living outside.

Little did I know that "Studied Casual," as I call it, is one of the hardest design ideas to carry off. These outdoor spaces and gardens have to feel right in the context of where they are, be appropriate for the people who inhabit them, and, hopefully, be so well designed and harmonious that the designer's hand is not apparent. I am not interested in a big "look at me" artistic statement, which distracts from a harmonious environment. My goal is to make gardens and parks that are tranquil outdoor places away from the chaotic, noisy, machine-driven environments where most of us work and live. Most of all I make beautiful places to be in love. I am a diehard romantic, but a practical one.

Very early in my life I decided that I wanted to make the world around me more beautiful, but my educational path and choices in the attempt may appear unconventional. As a young girl I would choose the scenic back road route, the most attractive house, the best-colored door, the best-looking clothes. I looked at everything. If it was ugly to me, I imagined ways to make it attractive. The road became lined with trees, our local eighteenth-century circle in a square center of town was restored to its original plan. Ugly new structures were torn down and rebuilt in a style that looked more appropriate. I planted little gardens around plain or shabby shacks and cottages, adding porches and vegetable gardens. I moved our house out in the country to overlook a pond filled with water lilies and alive with birds and wildlife. I planted vines and hedges to screen out ugliness and to create privacy. I planted trees for shade and soon learned that green leaves always make everything look better. In my mind I was always planting and painting everything.

At home I composed seasonal flowers and objects around the house. In doing the dinner table my brother and sister took turns with me: We were all visual, and Mother let us experiment with our ideas. We painted and repainted Mother's childhood playhouse inside and out, and I planted vegetables and flowers around it. Mother and I read garden catalogs and shelter magazines together, and had a running dialogue about what plants she would order. We were both seduced by blue flowers. She subscribed to a program at the Metropolitan Museum that delivered a new portfolio of famous paintings every month, and we took turns pinning them up in our rooms.

I loved the out of doors. I felt it was my own special place where I could really be me. I could roam the neighborhood and surrounding fields and woods; I just had to be home for dinner. First on foot, then on a bicycle, and then on my horse, I explored my environment. I learned that when I was on my own and had to take care of my own well being, I became totally alert, and sensitively aware of everything around me. I never came home clean; the out of doors is not tidy, and I had to get into the water, the mud, or the sand. My pockets were always full of my latest finds—a fallen bird's nest, shells. Once I brought home a pod secured to a stick with fine filaments. When the cocoon burst, my entire bedroom was covered in praying mantises.

Both my mother and my grandmother were good gardeners, but in different ways. Mother was obsessed with the health of her plants and the spectacular exotic blooms she could coax from her greenhouse plants, an exact reflection of herself. She was always unhappy about her garden—it was never perfect enough, something was always sick or wrong. She bought the latest chemicals promising perfection in her garden magazines. She rarely grew food, only a little lettuce in cold frames. Food was not her motivation, exotic plants and flowers were.

My grandmother was the opposite. She loved her house and her gardens. She had a huge organic kitchen garden, and everything she grew tasted much better than the produce from the supermarket.

She baked her own bread using organic stone ground wheat, and added seeds and dried fruits occasionally for fun and goodness. She preserved much of her produce: rows upon rows of beautiful fruit preserves, pickles, and the best tomato juice. She joyously shared her bounty with us and her neighbors. I loved my grandmother's approach to gardening and food.

My brother responded to my mother's desire for the unusual, the exotic, and the dramatic. It is not surprising that I became an outdoor designer, and he became a party planner and florist, building spectacular constructions and using exotic plants, though he was trained as an architect.

In the late forties, my parents hired modernist architects Victorine DuPont and Samuel Homsey to design and build a new house for us. Mother embraced the new. It was to be the exact opposite of the house where she grew up, full of light and air, not shrouded in layers of curtains and dark heavy materials. Watching this process—the sketches, the colored presentation drawings, the model, and the final blueprints—had a profound effect on me. I made little drawings of what I thought my room should be like, and where I wanted a tree.

After boarding school in Virginia, I choose Garland College in Boston so I could live in a city and because my best reading pal, Randy Williams, was going to Harvard. Later in life, his wife was to become my best friend, Bunny Williams, the noted interior designer and author, who wrote the foreword to this book.

At this finishing school, I had a mentor who told me about going to school abroad, and how I would have many adventures and learn much more about art and life. I remembered my mother's wistful lament about not being able to go to school in Switzerland because the war had broken out. I did not need much more encouraging. Off to Italy I went to another finishing school, the Villa Mercedes in Florence, where we studied art history and painting.

Florence was alive with art history, every view was famous, and I was electrified. I clearly learn best by experiencing and by doing. My design sensibilities were expanding, my depth of knowledge improving. I was no longer a simple country girl. I saw and tried to copy another more cultivated way of life. I was lucky to visit many private villas and gardens. Their memory is deep in my psyche and I draw on it regularly forty years later.

After a career in New York as an interior designer, I moved to California with my husband and small child. Wanting to work only part time, I scouted houses and gardens for magazines, what I called professional snooping, eventually becoming West Coast editor of *House Beautiful.*

And I could finally have my own garden. I immediately tore out part of the garden in our rental house. I removed those awful what I thought were cactus, *Agave attentuata*, and coarse birds of paradise, to build my eastern childhood garden. Little did I know that these strong plants would later become two of my favorites. I met my gardening mentor, Philip Chandler, a renowned plantsman and designer in a nursery. After I exclaimed, "These aren't the sages I know," he replied, "You haven't seen anything, honey, there are hundreds of sages in California." Like a puppy, I followed him around the nursery, and we became lifelong friends. I joined his plant identification class, a walking class around different neighborhoods where we saw plants and trees in all stages of life. I learned his preference for strong, healthy plants appropriate for our climate. I learned that when confronted with a sickly specimen, it was better to yank it out. "Wouldn't you rather watch a child grow than an old man withering away?" he asked (he was eighty at the time).

I had a lot of fun gardening in pots. Friends liked what I created, and asked me to help them with their pots. This was the beginning of a new career. Soon I joined an architectural designer, Tom Cox. In our new firm, he would do the architecture of the house and garden and I would do the plants, a classic collaboration. I soon realized that I had very strong opinions about both after we had designed my new house and garden. Some friends saw my new garden and we were asked to do one for them. The commute between Tom's Pasadena office and my house in Santa Monica became too much for both of us, so we parted. I realized I could hire designers to work with me, thus keeping a little bit of control. My natural friendliness and my garden attracted my first clients, and slowly my reputation grew.

I had been unfulfilled as an interior designer. Having seen many gardens while scouting for the magazines, I realized that there was a place for my ability to design spaces for living, but translated to the outside. I began building my plant and garden history library. My voracious reading habits were augmented by my desire to see the great gardens and outdoor spaces of the world. Over the years this quest has led to England, France, Spain, Germany, the Netherlands and Belgium; farther East to Persia, Bali, Java, Japan, Sri Lanka, Southern India, Australia, New Zealand; and to Brazil to see the great gardens of Roberto Burle Marx, who has influenced me a great deal with his patterning and love of bold native plants. Tracing the historical roots of garden making, I have seen and studied outdoor spaces, even some that are now ruins, trying to figure out how they were used, as well as carefully restored gardens.

Garden design is a living art form, the one field that brings together not only art and science, but also literature, history, mathematics, philosophy, and, for me, probably religion as well. I am attracted to sacred spaces and often find them in nature. Being outside makes me feel whole and vigorous. I can be very tense, anxious, and perhaps a little angry—what I call my trapped animal feeling. Then I go outside and the longer and deeper I go into wilderness the more this tension subsides. Soon I feel great.

Naturally I have become involved with the environmental movement, and have read its great philosophers: Thoreau, W. H. Hudson, John Muir, Aldo Leopold, Wendall Berry, Wes Jackson, and Michael Pollan. The more I read and learn, the more committed I am to helping the movement in every way I can, as we are in a crisis spiraling out of control in the destruction of our planet and of mankind.

First and foremost I am a proponent of sustainable practices indoors and out. For years I have followed appropriate gardening practices, planting drought-tolerant plants, promoting the beauty of native plants, using only organic seeds and heirloom varieties of fruits and vegetables for the kitchen garden, planting fewer lawns, and using only organic methods of fertilizer and pest management.

Making comfortable places to be outside for as many people as possible and turning asphalt playgrounds into schoolyard children's gardens have become the paramount missions of my studio. I feel that the garden has the ability to heal many of our society's educational problems, ills, and unhappiness, and I have always believed that one has to educate the little children first. I have experienced in person children's joyful response to discovering their first earthworm, and to eating vegetables they have planted, cared for, and cooked. I can see how something as intrinsically simple as a garden can transform their sad lives in so many ways.

My life's work was predicted when, at ten years old, I wrote in my baby book that I wanted to be a naturalist, a ballet dancer, a designer, and an army colonel. A garden designer combines all of these, tempered by all I have experienced. The field is humbling: You have to be a lifelong student because it is impossible to learn all the plants and how to use them. More importantly, like raising children, you never know, no matter how much you try, how your gardens will turn out. Your job designing, nurturing, and cherishing these living gardens brings never-ending joy and wonder.

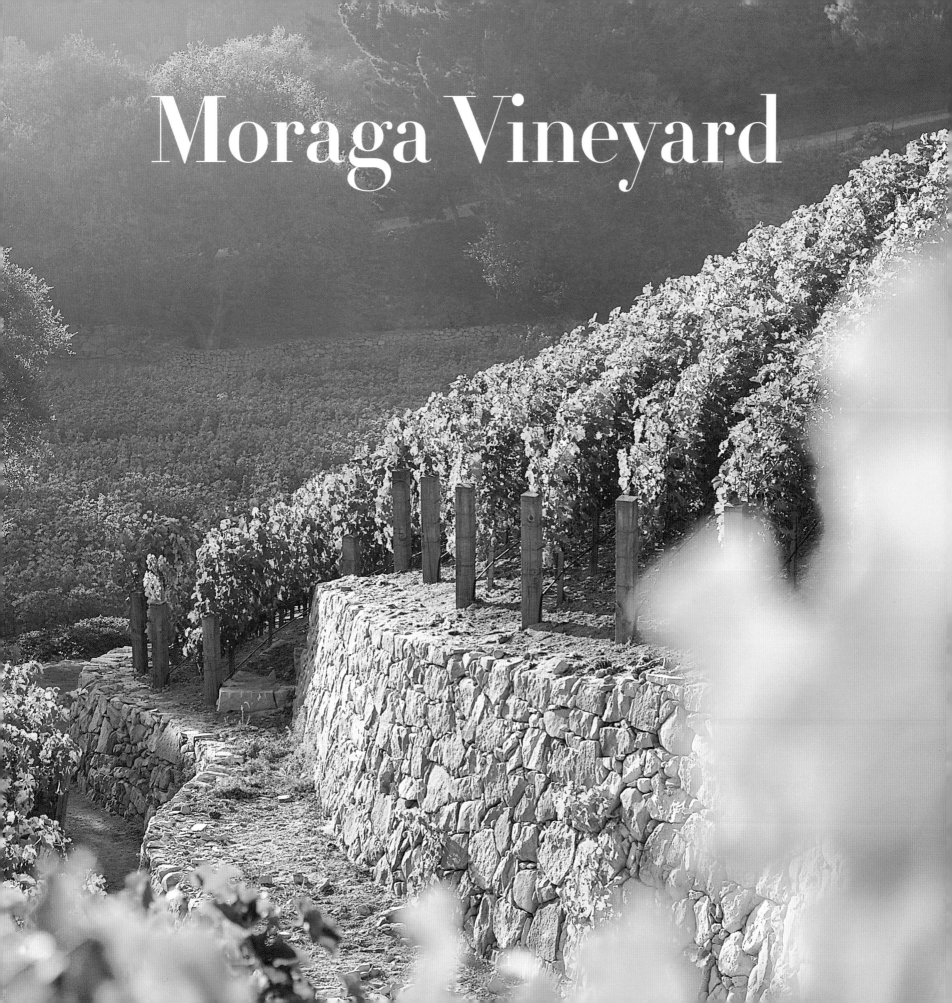

Moraga Vineyard

In 1980 my good friend Tom Buckley, an esteemed interior designer, asked me to plant some terra-cotta pots for his clients Ruth and Tom Jones. This was the beginning of the best professional relationship I could ever desire. The estate would become what is now the highly regarded and very private Moraga Vineyard. After working with the Joneses for a few years, making small changes to the garden and gaining their trust, I convinced them that we needed to create a master plan for the site. We began to build the architectural bones for the garden. We studied, planned, changed, and honed the site into what I consider to be my best garden.

and nasturtiums—but she wanted a garden with more order, one that was not as "messy." Tom was quite fond of the stone-terraced rows of grapevines and olive trees, and the kitchen gardens, of the agrarian landscape. Tom and I both had come from a long line of farmers and we shared a great love of the land and of growing our own food. My hope for the site was to make the house, garden, and vineyard completely cohesive. I chose an agrarian model based on traditional vine-growing regions with Mediterranean climates, rather than a suburban one that would reflect the vineyard's actual location.

Just minutes from busy Sunset Boulevard and the San Diego Freeway in the second largest city in the United States, the Joneses' agrarian paradise feels worlds away. The estate, tucked neatly and inconspicuously in Moraga Canyon in the Santa Monica Mountains, is located on a residential street lined with native sycamores, *Platanus racemosa*. The property is surrounded by a thick, pale ochre Santa Barbara sandstone wall covered by a Virginia

This agrarian paradise feels worlds away from Sunset Boulevard and the surrounding city

With soil and sunlight similar to that found in the gardens and vineyards of the great wine-growing regions the Joneses had visited in France—along with cool ocean breezes from the nearby Santa Monica bay—it seemed only natural that the Joneses would want to re-create the look and feel of the gardens they greatly admired in Italy and France. Ruth loved the flowers and the feeling of Giverny—the rows of bearded iris, the sunflowers

creeper (*Parthenocissus quinquefolia*) with leaves that repeat the shape of the sycamores'. There is no hint of the fourteen-acre vineyard and the three-acre gardens. The estate's entrance is graced by an old Mexican gate and bell, so discreet that they are easily overlooked. The gates that originally opened abruptly into the entrance court have been moved to the northern end of the property. Driving through the gates, one is struck by a dramatic, bright, and open view

Previous pages: *Morning light on a hillside of undulating stone terraces planted with grapevines and olive trees in the Santa Monica Mountains.*
Below: *Ground plan of the Moraga Vineyard.*

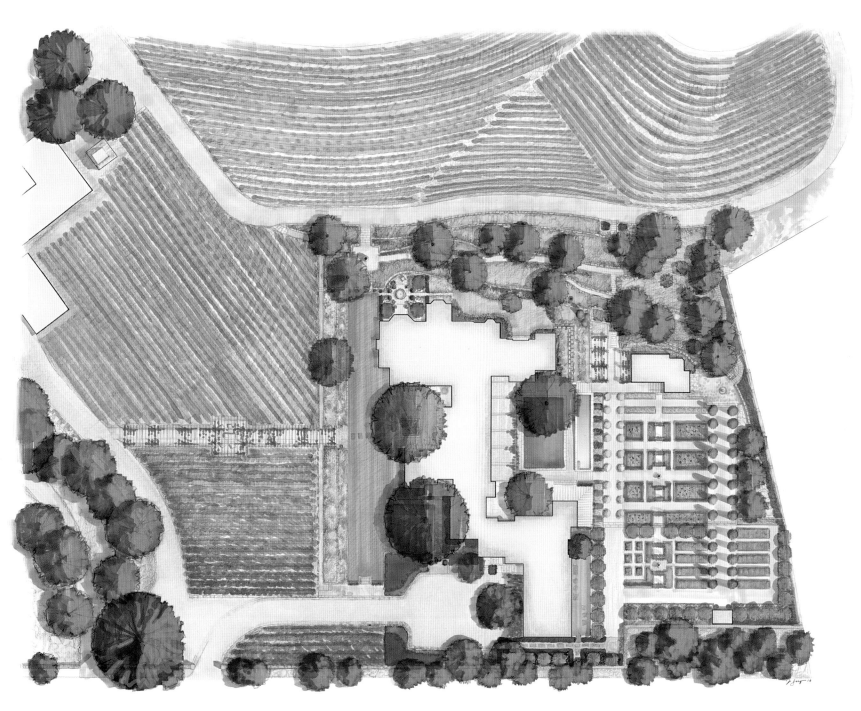

N

Clipped rosemary buttresses the swimming pool, built like a stone tank. Plump hassocks of gray germander line the decomposed gravel path. Handrails make the steep steps feel safe, while aromatic shrubs on both sides add sensory pleasure.

of vineyards that stretch up as far as the eye can see into the surrounding hillsides. You can't believe you are in the city.

The climate closely mimics that of Napa Valley: The same cool fog from the Pacific climbs up the canyons in late spring and early summer. Winters are cool and wet, with an annual rainfall of fifteen inches and an occasional frost. Long, dry summers provide an ideal climate for grapes to grow on vines covering the steep sides of the canyon. Deep alluvial soil has washed down the hill over the years, making rich soil for the house and garden at the bottom of the site.

Tom Jones has always enjoyed the process of designing and building. Trained as an aeronautical engineer, he ultimately became the CEO of Northrop Grumman Industries, where he

The house and its adjacent gardens were at the bottom of the hillside and longed for a better connection north to the hills. We created a pair of long stone staircases on either end. On the south side of the house the stairs climb east, up to the vineyard. This was the strongest site move I made.

Stone is plentiful in our local mountains and was one of the earliest building materials, so we chose stone as the chief unifying material for the site. All of the walls, terraces, paths, and, eventually, the new winery and wine-tasting cottage would be made of stone. What had been red brick ribbons running through the rose garden became decomposed gravel paths trimmed with stone edging, using local materials that related to the site. Even the chicken house, designed by Joe Sturges of my design team, had stone walls, which proved to be a good choice

Santa Barbara stone becomes the unifying material

strived to build the best airplanes possible. When the vineyard produced its first wine in 1989, he applied this same standard of excellence to the project, from the simplest ditch to the wine itself. Wine consultant Tony Soter was hired, along with his assistant at the time, Scott Rich, who is now Moraga's winemaker along with Mary Hall, the renowned Napa Valley vintner.

for keeping the rats out and keeping the coop cool in summer and warmer in winter. Paths were connected, vistas enhanced, and the stroll around the site became much easier and clearer to navigate on foot. The stone at the site served as the architectural spine of the garden; without good, clear bones, both the design and clarity of the garden are lost in unstructured plantings.

The farm manager, the late Roberto Quintana, found a local quarry, had huge boulders brought to the site, and set up a stone-cutting yard behind the barn. We discovered that one of the vineyard hands, David Rodriguez, had worked as a stonecutter in Mexico and had a good natural feel for stone. In fact, watching him decide where to start cutting the stone to avoid splintering it into a million pieces was much like watching a diviner find water. David cut every stone that we used on site. Stone is the best building material a region can provide, and using local stone resulted in architecture with a very natural feel, as if structures literally grew up from the ground.

Many of the young designers who have worked for me through the years have had the opportunity to work on Moraga. I always encourage design solutions and ideas from everyone on my team—although only the best are accepted. When the Joneses asked us to expand the house to include a new room for wine tasting, a young architectural designer in my studio, William Nicholas, became the project designer. Bill grew up in a nearby canyon. He was a meticulous designer, trained in fine arts and architecture at

There was much work to be done in the garden. The original swimming pool was bright turquoise and boomerang shaped. Since it was damaged by the Northridge earthquake in 1994, we removed it and replaced it with a raised swimming tank with an olive-ochre plaster bottom. Gentle water spouts that cross in the middle, inspired by pools at the Alhambra in Granada, Spain, provide the perfect place for the Joneses' grandchildren to play and dream up games of chance. A large cut-stone border serves as a high bench seat surrounding the pool.

Next to the pool is a perfect piece of sunken lawn framed by wide stone steps. Like a putting green, it was installed with great care over sand and gravel, so there is never a wet spot left on the lawn as any water drains immediately. It is always perfectly ready for their young granddaughters to enjoy or for Uva (grape in Spanish), the Joneses' beloved pug, to romp around with my pug, Lola. A deciduous tipu tree (*Tipuana tipu*), with soft gold flowers in spring, is placed off center on the lawn, providing light shade in the summer, colored leaves in the fall, and a lovely silhouette against the leafless vine-covered hills in the winter.

for the walls, terraces, paths, and winery buildings

Harvard, and I knew he could seamlessly add a new building to the older one. As a lover of wine, good food, and living well, I knew he would be perfect for the project. We soon discovered that from this new room you could survey much of the site, so we added a covered dining porch, which softens the house and shades it from the strong southern sun.

There is also a stone statue memorializing the first pug who roamed the vineyard.

What really transformed their entire courtyard, however, was the addition of a ten-foot plinth, raised to the level of the house. By building a pergola on stone columns, we created another outdoor dining space enhanced by lovely, soft dappled light filtering in through inexpensive bamboo fencing aged for covering. This courtyard and the terraces around it provide the best vantage points for observing the mesmerizing light on the hillside as it changes throughout the day from dawn to dusk and from one season to the next.

Ease of walking and climbing ensure safety, essential in any garden I build. I want the visitor's experience to be graceful, so the garden's beautiful flowers and trees can be enjoyed without worrying about what lurks underfoot. From the start it is vital to avoid anything that might make one nervous or fearful. In addition, comfort is important. For example, steep stairs should have no more than seven risers before there is a broader level to allow visitors to catch their breath, check out the view, and then continue on to another set of steps. This design sequence is a favorite that was inspired by a long set of stairs designed by Beatrix Farrand at Dumbarton Oaks in Washington, D.C. I also believe that handrails are quite useful when a stairway is really steep or precarious. At Moraga, I have tucked handrails into fragrant shrubbery so aromatic rosemary brushes gently against the climber's leg or hand as he or she uses the stairway. This pleasant sensory experience also helps one to forget just how steep the stairs are!

Subtle lighting on the path and stairs makes wandering around the garden at dusk or in the evening mysterious and romantic. Green shrubbery shapes become animals. The scents of gardenias and lavender are sweet, particularly on warm, humid evenings. One often encounters wildlife, and the deep bass of a great horned owl's hoot followed by the serenade of a mockingbird adds live music to the scene.

The rose garden is Ruth Jones's great pride and joy. Modeled on the rose garden at Bagatelle in Paris, their cutting garden provides Ruth with masses of roses to enjoy both inside her house and as she walks through the garden. When I first arrived at Moraga, one looked at the rose garden from a clumsy concrete Italianate balustrade, which had little connection with the building's ranch house feel. This garden was shaped like a football, used brick surrounded each flowerbed, and the colors of the blooms were randomly mixed. A lath house needing extensive repair and greenhouse wings were located behind the rose garden.

Left: *The original swimming pool and spa in a sea of red brick that needed to be replaced as it was damaged by the Northridge earthquake in 1994.* Opposite: *View over the new swimming pool, the rosemary buttresses, and the rose garden.*

Above: *Rampant roses contained by low hedges of dark green germander* (Teucrium chamaedrys) *with clipped balls of gray germander* (Teucrium fruiticans). Right: *The original football-shaped rose garden.* Opposite: *'Graham Stuart Thomas' roses cascade over copper arches to frame the view of an 18th-century oil jar.*

They housed orchids and had become a mortuary for plants, so it was an easy decision to remove the structures.

Roses do not have great legs and form, but they have beautiful heads in every color imaginable, so I decided to have an orthogonal design with a clear axis to help unify their unruly growing habits, grounding them with stone edging, dark green clipped *Teucrium*, and soft decomposed paths. The flowers were rearranged in a diagonal gradation of color, with white and the softest pinks and palest peaches placed in the front, followed by blooms of yellow, deep orangey peach, and finally, the dark rich burgundy color of

reworked. This bountiful garden supplies the table throughout the year with Beverly Hills and Anna espaliered apples (chosen for their ability to produce fruit with little or no frost), squash, beans, peas, many kinds of lettuce, herbs, and great tomatoes in the summer, and boysenberries, strawberries, and raspberries in early fall. Both the rose and the kitchen gardens have a dark green allée of Italian cypress (*Cupressus sempervirens*) as their backgrounds, which makes the roses and the vegetables really stand out.

Mutual trust and respect for the craftsmen on the job helped create a remarkable working environment in which each of us was

Viewing the rose garden in full bloom is like experiencing a living Impressionist painting

the Mr. Lincoln. Viewing the rose garden in full bloom from the porch is much like experiencing a living Impressionist painting. Over the years we have replaced roses that did not perform well along with old varieties that had become boring. The garden features many favorite hybrid teas, climbing roses, and the new David Austin roses, which are bred to resemble older varieties and carefully selected for beauty and stamina.

Like Ruth's rose garden, Tom's kitchen garden has also been

constantly inspired to give the best we had to offer. The results we achieved are indeed of a very high level of excellence. As a team, we would draw, make plans, discuss, and lay it out on the ground. Oftentimes we made a mockup out of plywood, adjusting and refining the plan as we built. Tom's engineering background helped him understand how things worked. With my strong sense of how everything needed to look and the great talents of our stonemasons, we formed a perfect team.

The sunroom and its porch, designed by
William Nicholas, offer views over the garden
and up to the surrounding vine-covered hills.

Above left: *Chartreuse globes of* Euphorbia characias wulfenii *contrast with gray serrated leaves of artichokes and boxwood balls.* Above right and opposite: *Iris 'Grandma's Purple Flag' is a midsize reblooming California favorite.* Left: *The original pool terrace.*

Above left: *Flowering plum and Spanish bluebells in the kitchen garden.*
Above right: *Beneath olive trees, tiny spring jonquils and antique freesias*
peek through snow-in-summer (Cerastium tomentosum).
Opposite: *Native oaks lightly shade California lilac* (Ceanothus griseus
horizontalis *'Yankee Point'*) *along a winding path across the hills.*

Previous pages, left: *Beneath the wisteria fringe an old Mexican barn door leads to the kitchen garden.* Previous pages, right: *Framed by low stone steps, the* tapis vert *provides dancing space for the Joneses' granddaughter.* Above: *Lady Banks roses* (Rosa banksii) *cover the roof of the garden shed. Nasturtiums have naturalized under the citrus trees, and kumquat standards in pots flank the antique painted door.* Opposite: *Ruth Jones often gives me a little basket of eggs from the vineyard's free-range chickens.*

Casa Nancina

Ten years ago, I found two derelict cottages, perched on an ancient sand dune a block from edgy Venice, in what I have nicknamed Baja Santa Monica. Recently divorced, with an eighteen-year-old son still at home, I thought I could live in the front cottage and the back one could become Oliver's *garçonnière*, the traditional New Orleans cottage for the young bachelor. That way we could be separate but close, a good living situation for this new stage in our lives: Oliver going to the local college, which was within walking distance, and I not very far from my studio and longing to start fresh alone. In my fifties, I was eager to explore and expand my professional interests, which had not jived with those of my husband, who was a film producer.

Dead plants and junk were everywhere on the property, and it felt very old and shabby. A hobby shop full of black widow spiders and long forgotten projects sat right in the middle of what I envisioned as a perfect courtyard. And the smell! The overpowering odor of a cathouse, reminiscent of the scent of old boxwood, which I remember hiding in as a child—familiar, but in this case not pleasant.

I thought, if I can't fix this up, no one can. It is just a nondescript white box. Clean it up a bit, paint it bright colors, add some French doors . . . et voilà! A home I can live with until Oliver goes away to university and I can find something I like better.

It initially spoke to me because it was high above the street and less than a mile from the ocean, with a great breeze, in a changing neighborhood. I never like to be too far from the ocean as it reminds me of my childhood summers at the beach in Delaware, and I enjoy walking on the beach at dawn or dusk. Located perhaps a little too close to the worst street in Santa Monica, the neighborhood was more lively and colorful than my former solidly tidy middle class street. Pier Avenue still had a few shacks and badly neglected cottages like mine on it, although several had been "done up" and gentrified. Most of the cottages were small and close to the street, which meant that everyone was always spilling out onto the sidewalk. Garage doors were always open, revealing guys (including my son) working on old cars or mothers huddled over washing machines doing the weekly laundry; small children played on the sidewalks; friendly dogs out in the yard greeted everyone in hopes of a kindly pat on the head; and, of course, one very tidy neighbor polished his cars, sprayed his walls, and served as the self-appointed master of our garbage cans.

I immediately started making sketches and site plans of what I wanted in my new house. I knew that the center of this tiny house (1,500 square feet) was to be a keeping room—one-half kitchen and one-half sitting room with a fireplace—spilling onto a central patio between the two cottages. Plus there would be a serene bedroom where I could hear the sound of the fountain immediately below my balcony and shuttered doors; a "big room," a flexible space for dining, dancing, and for reading in the sunny morning window; and a loggia where I could read, dine, and entertain outside. Being close to the ocean, I knew I would need a fireplace outside to cozy up to when the marine fog came in. Because of our mild Mediterranean climate of hot dry summers and cool, sometimes rainy winters, I could dine and entertain outside in front of a fireplace.

The cottage was a white stucco box of no particular style tucked into a hill and hidden from the street. I needed to decide in which direction to take the house. I have always been torn between the classic modern house and the local Spanish-influenced adobe style, which I call the cult of Ramona, after a novel written by Helen Hunt Jackson in 1884, which romanticized a picturesque view of the early life on a Spanish land grant rancho in Southern California. In the case of the former I could have remodeled it based on a nearby 1919 Irving Gill apartment complex: modern, clean, simple white stucco with corner windows, with few details. Or, of the latter, as a colorful courtyard-facing tile-roofed casita full of charm, which I decided would sell better.

Traveling has become my university education; I have little college education. My first experience was two years in the early sixties studying art and architecture in Florence, where I became a born-again Italian. Extensive travel has given me the opportunity to experience "spaces" all over the world and to study how people use them. I gravitate toward other Latin cultures and climates because they relate best to Southern California. It is logical that I would pull ideas from my most memorable trips to help me decide how to attack the remodel.

Naturally, Southern Spain's Andalusia was first, as so much of the architecture had been brought to California by the

Previous pages, left: *I am happy working in the garden.* Previous pages, right: *The central courtyard garden between my keeping room and the* garçonnière, *shown at the top of the plan* (this page).

early Spanish settlers. In the early nineties, my associate, Wade Graham, an environmental writer and designer, and I managed to go to Andalusia on the way to a job I was doing with Frank Gehry in Germany. I had been studying books written in the twenties with measured drawings of gardens and buildings, trying to figure out what the spaces were like, so I made the most of the trip. We stayed at the edge of the Alhambra in Granada, and soaked in the magic of that most romantic place, as well as photographing every fountain detail. These memories were the strongest ones I drew from to design my house.

Another trip, to Brazil, opened up my eyes to the poetic colonial Portuguese house and garden when I visited Roberto

Brazil's plants made me want to see more tropical paradises. When I received an invitation to a bamboo conference in Bali, I accepted immediately. Wade and I attended the conference, held in Ubud, Bali, to learn more about tropical plants, sustainability, and design. Bali was richer culturally and spiritually than anywhere I had ever been. The Balinese were in touch with the land, created beautiful sacred spaces in temples, and spent much of their lives honoring the land and its spirits. The tropical foliage, the rice paddies, the humid climate made living outside appealing—just a little open pavilion was needed.

My painting group, the Santa Monica Watercolor Society, planned a trip to Morocco. Again I jumped at the opportunity.

The rich exposure to so many cultures bubbled up in the design of my new home

Burle Marx's estate outside of Rio. His house was so exciting and it showed me that a colonial building could become more modern and bohemian. It didn't have to be a pastiche of the eighteenth century. The garden was even more dramatic, with sweeps of native plants, bold colors, and exuberant foliage. I didn't have to have formal eighteenth-century clipped parterres and obvious straight axes with center fountains in the crossings, which can be traced back to Persia through Islamic Spain and Portugal. I could be wild, and paint with plants as I felt he did. Fountains were everywhere, dripping through large carved rocks like the natural ones in the rugged terrain of Brazil. The New World's exotic tropical plants replaced overly familiar Old World flora.

More Islamic gardens, date groves, and a climate like that of California were beckoning me, the classic romantic. This was to be the last trip before finding my little shacks.

It is no surprise that this rich exposure to so many cultures and design ideas bubbled up in the design of my new home. I did a small watercolor of what I romanticized as the cottage of a dashing Brazilian, the illegitimate son of a rich landowner. He was the overseer of his father's estates and of course we had fallen in love. He called the cottage Casa Nancina. I thought about all of the sensual experiences I wanted to have in this house with him and alone, and my design was based on this.

I painted the tiny cottage white with deep saffron trimmed

Above: *My watercolor sketch with colors inspired by a monastery in Brazil, showing what I dreamed my little cottage could become.* Left: *The original cottage without the old foundation planting, just as I began to transform it.*

windows and a saffron dado around the bottom of the house and a border around the top. I tore open a small packet of saffron I had brought home from Morocco and mixed it with water to get a full grasp of this color, which I had seen used so exquisitely in Seville, Spain, and Ouro Preto, Brazil. It looked beautiful against the sky, and also worked equally well with terra-cotta and the grays and verdant foliage I wanted to plant in my garden.

I wanted Casa Nancina to reveal herself slowly. On the street level, my neighbor Bob's front hillside was filled with agaves (*Agave attenuata*) and Christmas candelabra aloes (*Aloe arborescens*), which have huge torchlike red blossoms at that season, so I marched them across the front of my property adjacent to the sidewalk. I added trailing rosemary, Matilija poppies, and ceanothus. I didn't want my landscape to stand out. It needed to be discreet and feel as if it belonged to the neighborhood.

With that in mind, I retained the existing first set of cement stairs, and continued the path in stone. It is now edged with a clipped upright rosemary hedge on both sides—my homage to the formal garden! The first terrace rises above the walk, and is hedged with clipped juniper. A friendly red front gate with an open grill frames the pebble path alongside the house and the stairs leading to the front porch. By the time you have arrived here you have been able to change your public high alert, rubbed against the rosemary, have hopefully started to respond to the sensual smells surrounding you, and heard the trickling of a fountain.

Casa Nancina framed by my favorite agave (Agave attenuata). Matilija poppies looking like fried eggs pop up through ceanothus, aloes, and rosemary.

Inside the gate you find yourself under a giant California fan palm (*Washingtonia filifera*) and a favorite dragon tree (*Dracaena draco*). A messy and unpopular red bottlebrush (*Callistemon citrinus*) completes the quirky palate of trees I inherited on the property. I love them and all they bring to the garden: shade, shape, color, history, and endurance, as they survived the early neglect and the remodel. They have become homes and nourishment for all kinds of wildlife.

The house peers down on the front courtyard, revealing a geometric-patterned stone terrace, a wall fountain, and a small table and chairs perfect for my morning coffee. William Nicholas, an architect working for me at the time, helped me make my plans

bedroom above the terrace; they bloom at different times of the year. The smell of jasmine wafting in all year around . . . imagine how this was for an East Coast girl!

The forgotten spaces in most people's houses—the side yards and setbacks—I look at as opportunities. I paid a lot of attention to the narrow walkway that runs along the eastern side of the house. I had my favorite mason, José Aguirre, lay smooth brown stones on their edge in a herringbone pattern, which directs energy to the center patio; periwinkle wisteria and thunbergia hang over the ochre walls. The wall casts its warm golden glow into the house at all times of the day. I put a niche in the wall so that I'd always have something to look at from inside the living room. I have

A feathery and rare Kashmir cypress casts a soft shadow on the courtyard

work. He designed the terrace, basing it on a ceiling in the Palazzo Ducale in Urbino, with which I was also familiar. The fountain is an adaptation of one that I saw and actually measured in the courtyard of an eighteenth-century townhouse in Ouro Preto, Brazil. A feathery and rare Kashmir cypress (*Cupressus cashmeriana*) casts a soft shadow on the fountain and courtyard, blocking the intense western sun and my neighbors' large house. The cypress is one of a group that I had grown for the Norton Simon garden and is very dear to my heart. Burmese honeysuckle climbs the house and anything else she can get her greedy fingerly tendrils around. The sweet fragrance from her long golden trumpets wafts into my bedroom and is joined by two jasmines also growing up and onto the balcony and into my

always been very in tune with the seasons and cycles of life, so I add seasonal touches all around the garden: weird pumpkins in the fall, poinsettias at Christmas—this is where they really look fabulous—paperwhites and bulbs in the spring, small ferns or cool colored coleus in summer. I thought carefully about what I would see and hear from every window of my little house and gave each a focal point. It is an ongoing art project.

The center patio is a perfect extension of the house, a space in which I spend a huge amount of time puttering, daydreaming, eating,

A fountain tinkles under my balcony window shaded by a Kashmir cypress (Cupressus cashmeriana).

Above left: *Pots of Catalina chalk dudleya line the shelf along the stairs to the front porch.* Above right: *A close-up of their chalky faces.*
Opposite: *Burmese honeysuckle fills my bedroom with tropical fragrance.*

entertaining, reading, and, most important, napping. I call the plum-colored banquette my napatorium. I encourage my friends to fall asleep in every chair, chaise, or sofa the way my friends did when I was a teenager in my family's house on the beach. A little nap after a long lunch with wine before my guests drive back to their own homes is offered with very soft throws to take care of the afternoon chill.

This patio and garden has a lot going on yet doesn't feel busy or nervous. I know that the more you define a space, the larger it becomes. Water trickles from little bronze Javanese tigers into the central pond with an attached Jacuzzi spa. I designed the water to be seen all the way through the house and make a strong central axis that pulls you outside. The water also helped organize the adjoining spaces, making them seem calm and orderly. The jungle created by the wild tropical plants coming right up to the edge of the terrace and pond is enhanced by the uncertainty of not knowing where the garden begins or ends. That illusion was achieved by painting the west wall of the garden and the back of the fountain the same cobalt blue I had seen in the Majorelle garden in Marrakech, where I had done a watercolor.

My watercolor of a dream pond (above) *and its realization* (opposite), *with what I call "Las Damas de Noche," a double datura, hanging over the spa with her seductive fragrance permeating the evening.* Left: *The dilapidated shack I made into a garçonnière for my son. The little building's wall became the backdrop for the fountain and pond, which can be seen through the entire house.*

The existing giant schefflera, an overgrown houseplant to my East Coast eyes, set the tropical design direction for the garden surrounding the patio. The schefflera grows right into my neighbor's giant ficus trees to the west that form a dense British racing green boundary. It has become the perfect background for the chartreuse tree ferns I planted as the middle ground in a plane of native ferns, daniella, hellebores, geraniums, fragrant gingers, and mat-forming campanulas. I have tried to include plants with blue flowers and all the shades of green. Giant dark blue agapanthus mimic the cobalt walls. An exotic and seductive cream datura hangs over the spa. Its heady nighttime perfume makes the spa even more sensual. For drama and interest, I tuck

appropriate to our marine climate. Once in a while they grow, other times they just wither. It is not an easy place to garden, since the courtyard has limited sun and air circulation, and we often have fog. But to be a gardener you have to be an optimist and keep trying. A perfectionist by nature will never be a happy gardener, as it is impossible to control nature: It is alive and always changing, living and dying when it wants to. I think that is why I am happier being a garden designer than I was as an interior designer: I celebrate changes and know that anything alive is messy like me.

I love the idea that all my senses are always engaged in my garden. It's a totally sensual experience—the aroma of rosemary as

I think of my garden as a living theater with a different show every season

dark blue glazed pots filled with fragrant hot pink lilies and maiden-hair ferns native to the local mountains into the lush greens. They remind me of Diana Vreeland's remark that pink was the navy blue of India. I adore dark blue and hot pink. Exotic bulbs from the Mediterranean climates of the world are placed all around in the garden for another dramatic effect in the dappled light. They all need a dry season, so I keep them on the side of my house until they are ready to show off. The colors of amaryllis, Roman hyacinths, freesia, ornithogalum, and leucojums make my garden a living theater with a different show every season.

On the sunny side I grow plants for making salads: mesclun, arugula, mint, basil, tarragon, Japanese eggplant, and tomatoes

you brush against it coming up the front steps, the burbling bells of water in the fountain, the fuzzy texture of peppermint geranium (*Pelargonium tomentosum*) begging to be rubbed, the rustle of the king palm's fronds, and the deep deep bongs of the big timber bamboo as the trunks bang against each other. And I never tire of the ever-changing light, the subtle shadows created by the intermittent sunlight streaming through the foliage and ferns reflected on the saffron wall, the warm light bouncing through the house, or bamboo patterns on my crisp white linen bed curtains.

Miss Lily has a drink from Lily's Pond and watches a cat TV show of orange goldfish.

Above left and right: *A path of river stones set in a herringbone pattern transforms the once dreary narrow alley,* left, *that connects the back courtyard with the barn-red gate,* opposite.

Above: *I have always had pink living rooms, so I painted my outdoor living room pink as well, and added a contrasting saffron wall. In my favorite sixties combination of chartreuse green and pink, the leaves of 'Fenway', a* Parthenocissus, *create a tracery on the wall.* Left: *A smelly hobby shop was replaced by a covered porch with fireplace.* Opposite: *The covered porch, with an outdoor sink and drinks tray, is always ready for friends. The French doors lead to the kitchen.*

Harte Garden

Spectacularly sited on a hill just above the famed San Ysidro Ranch in Montecito, Anne and Houston Harte's house and garden face south toward breathtaking views of the Pacific and the Channel Islands and north toward the Los Padres Mountains. Though the views were breathtaking, the clients wanted a better fit between their house and gardens, more flat space for the children, and gardens that were easier to maintain. They asked me to help them develop the remaining property, which had rudimentary landscaping but a great porch and swimming pool below.

The handsome house, designed by Bob Easton and finished in 1989, is a contemporary version of an adobe house with very thick dusky terra-cotta pink plaster walls. The interiors have high ceilings, wooden beams, and generously scaled rooms, perfect for the dramatic location. The Hartes' love of Mexico—Anne has a shop in San Miguel de Allende—is reflected in both the architecture and the furnishings of their house.

In the garden I tried to emulate Anne's bold use of color, scale, and texture. Their garden couldn't be filled with dainty flowers and plants. It needed sweeps of color and strongly architectural plants.

Nor could it be chopped up into small garden rooms; they had to be ample and to include varied experiences.

We worked very closely with the Hartes on the master plan for the property. The entrance sequence was made more enticing by adding an allée of olive trees. I felt that the high stone wall needed the scale of those trees to mediate the two levels, disguise the garage entrance, soften the light, and add shade to the large expanse of parking. We added gravel and decomposed granite to make the drive feel less formal. Their talented stonemasons, Antonio and José Sarabia, built new stout stone columns to flank a simple rustic gate.

Every stonemason has his own artistic style in the way he works stone. Antonio's is very bold; he loves large stones, and fits them together in the most imaginative ways. He proved to be just right for this property. A mason who carefully measures and makes tight geometrical walls would not have been appropriate here.

We placed my trademark agaves (*Agave americana*) in the gravel. As they are more than five feet tall and wide, they feel like giant modern sculptures. Agaves have been repeated around the garden to make the house seem as if it were tucked into a large patch of agaves in the local hills. They seem to tumble diagonally down the hillside. One giant, very overscaled agave inhabits a small courtyard. The agaves are underplanted with California native ceanothus below an orchard of olive trees high on the hillside. The mass planting is broken by a small stone arroyo seco, its edges lined with a ribbon of iris in early spring. During the winter rainy season the arroyo gushes with rainwater from

House and garden face south to the Pacific and the

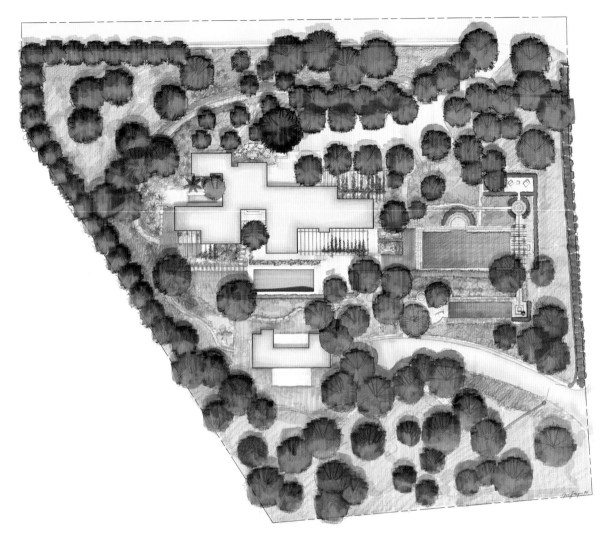

Channel Islands, north to the Los Padres Mountains

the hills above, making its way down the canyons to the sea.

With the native chaparral adjoining the property, I felt it was necessary to repeat the grays and dark olive greens, with small touches of light purple blues—the color of the mountains late in the day. Then, nearer the south-facing terraces, colors would slowly grade to strong, bright, more tropical colors. Anne had already planted huge containers of bright geraniums, hibiscus, and bougainvillea in orange, hot pink, and magenta. After we planted the terrace pergola with giant Burmese

Previous pages, left: *Bleeker and Gracie greet guests as they arrive at Anne and Houston Harte's garden in Montecito.* Previous pages, right: *A pergola against the Los Padres National Forest in the Montecito foothills.* Above: *Ground plan of the Harte Garden.*

Above left: *The outdoor sitting room's fireplace, where you can warm up for a cozy conversation and a glass of wine.* Left: *The lawn after it had been graded flat and before the stairs were built.* Opposite: *Graceful steps for gliding between the pool terrace and the big lawn.*

honeysuckle (*Lonicera hildebrandiana*) and changed the materials of the furniture cushions to brighter fabrics, it became even more festive.

Working on this project, I began to think about the stages in one's life and how they can be reflected in one's garden. We terraced the hillside, which included one "event" lawn, big enough to play domestic ballgames, have a wedding or party, or romp with the dogs. The long stone wall on the west side is two-tiered, creating a bench that can be used to watch the ocean or the activity on the lawn, or become a platform for a small performance. Recalling how often I had strung cables from the house to provide electricity in such a situation, we remembered to put electrical outlets nearby. Outdoor electrical outlets are important, if you think about needs like heaters, Christmas lights, lights for parties, microphones and speakers for music, or any other equipment. Knowing how to plan for the ways an outdoor space may be used is one of our jobs.

At the end of the lawn we placed a pergola connecting two small enclosed gardens: one a dark room with hedge walls and a hammock in the center, the other a place for smaller ladylike plants, which would be lost in the main parts of the garden. In the first garden a small, low stone fountain carved by Antonio and surrounded with iris fills the center. From the fountain water runs through a rill under the pergola and tumbles down the center of the staircase, carefully lining up with the mountain peak on Santa Cruz Island, considered sacred by the local Chumash tribe.

The rill ends in another fountain on a terrace bordered by *Agapanthus* 'Storm Cloud'. We were lucky to find material the exact periwinkle blue for the two iron benches from 16 Solano in Mexico. Monterey cypress frame the view and block the tennis courts next door. We repeated the coral tree (*Erythrina*) on this terrace. Up by the pergola Antonio built a stone bench around an old oak tree, and formed an *horno*, a Mexican oven similar to a pizza oven. Next to it is a very simple grill. Eating in this intimate outdoor room under the coral and oak trees is very pleasant on warm evenings.

This is a garden that has places for quiet contemplation, reading, or bird watching, and on the final terrace below, probably the most active and interesting, there are cutting gardens for roses, a vegetable garden, a small orchard, and Houston's agave nursery. He collects the pups, small shoots that grow at the bottom of the plant, and plants them. They become fine specimens. Antonio is also the gardener, and he propagates lavender, knowing that it has a several-year lifespan and he will be ready with new plants when they die back.

Water gently bubbles up from a carved stone in the center of a pebble mosaic circle and trickles down a rill that is lined up with the highest peak on Santa Cruz Island, sacred to the Chumash tribe.

Above left: *Lion's tail
(Leonotis leonurus) blooms
all through summer and fall.*
Above right: *Water runs
down lavender-lined steps
into a deep well, taming
a formerly steep hill,* left.
Opposite: *Chaises look
over a lawn framed by
'Storm Cloud' agapanthus
to the mountains beyond.*

Above: Opuntia *cactus loom over stepping-stones to the guesthouse.*
Opposite: *The decomposed granite terrace is shaded by a gigantic coral tree.*

Above: *Stairs copied from those designed by Beatrix Farrand at Dumbarton Oaks in Washington, D.C., flanked by Christmas candelabra aloes* (Aloe arborescens) *that bloom for winter solstice.* Left: *A "before" view of the hillside with olives.* Opposite: *Olives are underplanted with ceanothus and punctuated by sculptural agaves.*

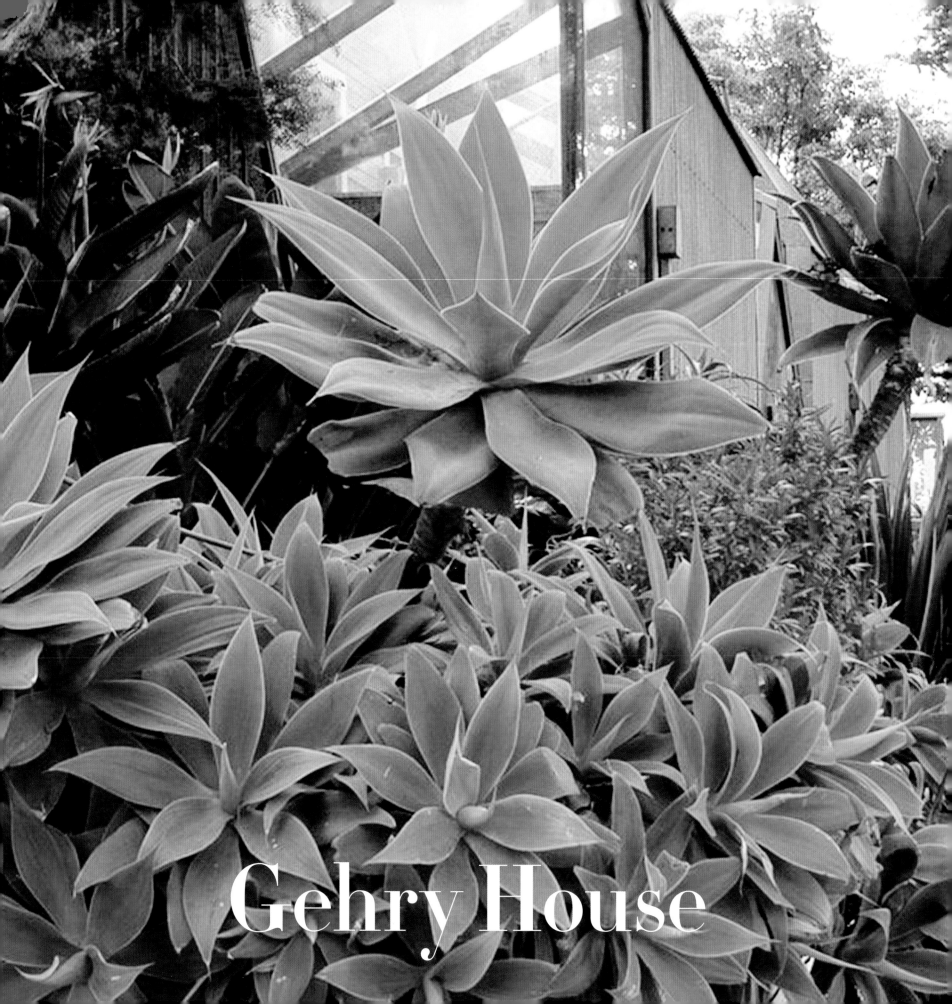

Gehry House

Frank Gehry called me one day more than twenty years ago and said in desperation, "Will you help me? They keep looking at me." I had no idea what he was talking about.

I had been to the Gehrys' house, near our house, many times to pick up my son, Oliver, who had become a friend of his son, Alejo, and had noticed that there was no garden, only dirt completely exposed to the street. Naively, I did not think that it was intentional. I figured that as I had left my front garden barren a long time because I had to earn the money to create it, he had done the same—normal for our two professions.

Finally, Frank explained that he had walked out of his house one recent morning in his pajamas, completely disheveled after a frisky Saturday night party, to pick up his Sunday *Times*, and heard a weird click-click sound. He turned around to face a dozen young Japanese architecture students who had come to photograph his famous revolutionary remodel of his suburban house and, as their luck would have it, him.

He had turned one of the city's ubiquitous little stucco boxes inside out, exposed the inner structure of the house down to its wiring, added cockeyed windows and chain link fencing. Asphalt paving ran through the kitchen and back outside. These bold moves were shocking to many people. Using these common materials, he had gotten the extra room and the additional light that he had wanted, and he hadn't spent much money to transform the house into what would later be considered an iconic work of art.

Frank wanted me to plant his adoring fans out, and my guess was that the astonished conventional neighborhood probably wanted this "junkyard," as many of them called it, of a house removed from sight. As one of his neighbors told me when I was planting Frank's garden, "He's ruined our neighborhood and devalued our properties."

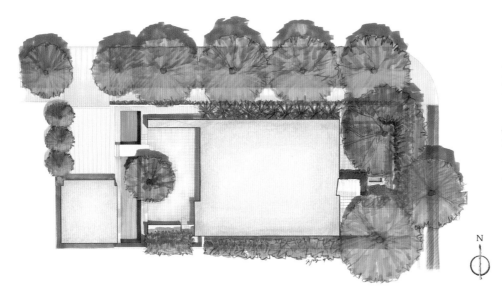

Previous pages, left: *Bronze flax,* Phormium tenax *'Atropurpureum', is a strong contrast to the house's galvanized siding.* Previous pages, right: *Responding to Gehry's architecture, agaves* (Agave attenuata) *and birds of paradise* (Strelitzia) *tumble over the wall onto the sidewalk, concealing a hidden terrace adjoining the kitchen.* Left: *Ground plan of the Gehry house and garden.*

As with any new garden, my first questions when designing Frank's garden were: What does the architecture have to say to the garden? Is it grounded or does it relate poorly to its site? How do I relate this property to the surrounding context? Where are the doors and windows of the house? How do you get in and out, and what do you see when you look out the windows? Do the clients want and need privacy? Where are they going to have outside living areas? Close to the kitchen? What are the practical needs: garbage, mail, lights? What are the climatic restraints on the site—sun, shade, light, wind, noise, wild animals?

I talked to Berta and Frank about what they would like to have, and asked about their childhoods. What were their favorite plants? Berta grew up in Panama with lush tropical foliage, whereas Frank grew up in Toronto—and in the end they compromised. I picked plants that have become part of California's cultural landscape, plants that I call workhorses: aloes, agaves, birds of paradise, Hollywood junipers, jade plants, green phormiums, green saucer aeoniums, rosemaries, yuccas, dracenas. They are strong, perform without fuss, and have great bones and shapes.

I walked around our neighborhood and observed older houses with neglected gardens. What was still alive and surviving vigorously? Aloes, for example, with vibrant flowering red candlabras splendid at Christmastime and twisted, spiky foliage, look good year after year. These plants became dominant in my designs. At the time, the early eighties, they were not in fashion. Everyone had just discovered white 'Iceberg' roses and lavender, which were replacing azaelas, impatiens, camellias, and tree ferns.

What I picked was exactly the opposite of this new, soft, spineless palette. These, too, are good plants, but they need strong, ordered, dark, solid shrubs, often tightly clipped, to create structure and show off their intrinsic gentle beauty—light against dark.

For Frank and Berta's garden my workhorse plants provided the privacy they needed and they were easy to grow with little tending. I pulled the low wall in the front garden out to the street and added another wall six feet back, then filled the space with dirt, raising the plantings to provide almost immediate privacy. In the small terrace that was left, I planted a melaleuca (*Melaleuca linarifolia*), which reached up to the second floor, and I suggested they add a door to the kitchen.

Though Frank often complained to me and to my friends that I had done a lousy job, that his garden wasn't growing and that architectural groupies could still see him, I usually laughed, knowing one can't control plants, and told him to be patient.

One evening near Christmas, I was asked to dinner at their house and I brought Frank an automatic water tommygun and told him, "Shoot the nosy, rude lookie-loos through the few holes in your plantings. Maybe that will discourage them until the garden grows in!"

In the first years, Frank added a small water element with tongue-in-cheek kitchen fixtures and a couple of chairs to the terrace. Best of all, there was now a great breeze through the house when the door was open from the kitchen. Frank could bring a glass of wine out while Berta was preparing dinner and play with his water gun and Shar-Pei dogs—man and dogs having fun shooting and barking at the neighbors walking by. His neighbors now brag that he lives on their street, and the property values have jumped over the moon.

Schnabel Garden

an you imagine designing an English garden for a Frank Gehry house? How was I to interpret Marna Schnabel's wishes? Frank had always used either decomposed granite or a sea of green lawn around his buildings. Like most architects he preferred the building to stand alone as if it were a temple. Here were two diametrically opposed solutions to the site, with me in the middle. When I asked Marna more questions, I realized that she wanted a garden, not just plain dirt or a field of grass, and that she would have to talk Frank into having a garden.

When people want an English garden they are responding to contain architecturally strong plants with bold colorings and grass, bringing both camps together.

My inspiration came from a black-and-white photograph of yuccas, cordylines, and agaves against a stark white wall somewhere in the desert. This image was from a 1931 book that was one of my earliest influences and continues to inspire me, *California Gardens* by Winifred Starr Dobyns. The book has photographs of garden elements and details: terraces, stairs, pools, fountains, pergolas. I learned how earlier designers had handled the climatic conditions of the California landscape to make comfortable outdoor spaces.

I still lean toward classic solutions for California gardens. Mediterranean enclosed gardens are perfect for our climate of wet and dry seasons, with cool nights and warm days. Walled gardens offer so many solutions still relevant in the modern world. They give privacy and safety from the outside environment,

Enclosed gardens are perfect for our climate

the full, voluptuous, sprawling quality of a garden full of flowers, mostly roses, soft pastels, and plants with lots of fine texture. The picture of pink roses, the most feminine of flowers, trying to climb up the titanium structure kept coming up in my mind, and the absurdity still makes me giggle. I knew I had to adapt this English ideal to stand up to the building: A saccharine approach would not work here. If I screened the neighboring houses and telephone poles and framed the white structures and bold titanium center, they would be even more striking. The remaining site would often perceived as hostile. The living spaces of the house open onto exterior spaces, and outdoor dining is possible in courtyards in good weather most of the year. The celebration of water in fountains and pools provides both cooling in summer heat and decorative delight. It masks the sounds outside the garden. Garden walls, which keep small children and dogs safe in the garden, also make good surfaces for vines and shrubs, both edible and decorative. This model can be adapted for a contemporary building as well as a traditional one.

The Schnabel compound contains several pavilions connected by covered walks, stairs, and courtyards. The design was ideal for a family with three lively teenagers and dynamic parents. Ambassador Schnabel, recently back from Finland, had his study in the front, the quietest pavilion, looking into an olive orchard. One daughter had an apartment over the garage, another on the second floor; the master quarters overlooked a Finnish-inspired lake one story down. Their son Evan, a student and later an architect like his mother, was a wild drummer, so he had his own pavilion. They all gathered in the main house kitchen and living rooms.

Marna had worked for Frank Gehry after she went back to architecture school. They worked carefully together to come up with a brilliant modern adaptation of this very sophisticated and ancient concept of family pavilions in a compound surrounded by walls.

This was my first experience with Frank, and I was very impressed by his openness in allowing plants to enter his domain. I relished the idea of working with such strong architecture and I responded with equally strong plants that had architectural shapes, and interwove smaller textures around them to set them off even more. This layering of texture and color with strong shapes became one of the core elements of my design philosophy.

Previous pages: *Linked stucco-clad pavilions and a titanium-clad tower compose Frank Gehry's design for the family compound. Setting them off are pools, lawns, and strong plants.* Right: *Ground plan of the Schnabel Garden.*

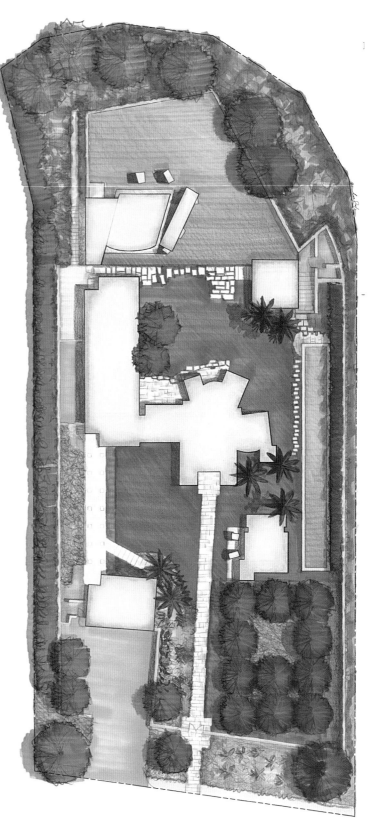

Left: *This black-and-white image of a planting by Ralph Cornell in Winifred Starr Dobyns' 1931 classic work,* California Gardens, *was my inspiration for the layered plantings of the Schnabel border,* above. Opposite: *Palms in the neighboring garden repeated next to the pavilion make the enclosed garden seem more expansive.*

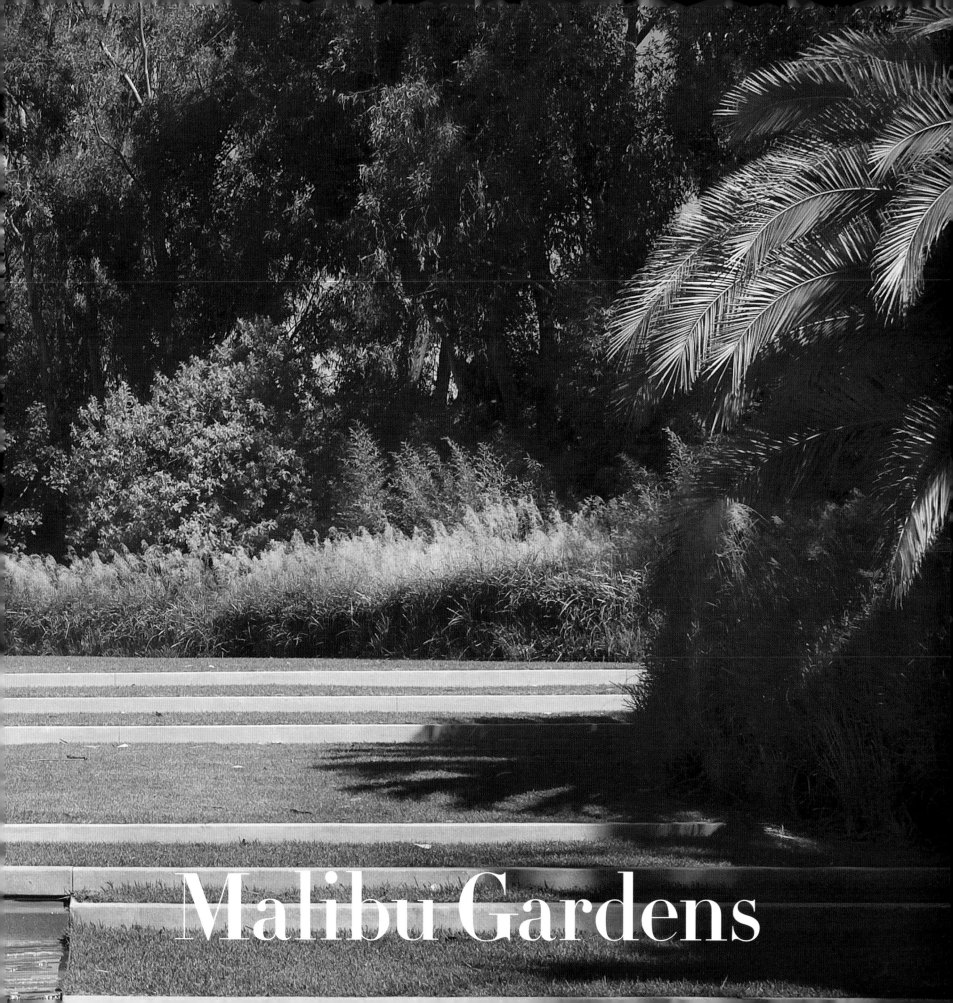

Malibu Gardens

With only the gentle sounds of waves breaking below, my client looks out past gently swaying beach grasses to a view of the Pacific Ocean from his bed. His only decision is whether to get up and go down to the beach to surf, or to cover his head and go back to sleep. For someone who has surfed all over the world, having your house and garden overlooking the best surfing spot in Malibu is a dream come true.

This was the third garden I had done for this client. The property was sensational, but the house was a shell with an undefined skeletal framework. One could see the potential, but we

within walking distance of the residential architecture of Richard Neutra, Craig Ellwood, and Cliff May.

For both of us, this very special project was a dream come true as well. We had grown up by the ocean on opposite coasts, and we both had dreamed of the perfect beach house. The next best thing for us was being able to design one for a special client who had the same spiritual connection to the powerful ocean.

The house would not be a pastiche of mid-century design, then experiencing a renaissance all over the country, but an updated version that was much more spacious and luxurious than the small, economical early modern houses.

The relationship to the outdoors is one of the essential qualities of the classic modern house, as are the spectacular, light-filled rooms. Attuned to the casual style of beach living, the owners decided to cook, dine, and live in one main room, emphasizing its amazing views of the Pacific. Working closely with

For one who has surfed all over the

needed an architect who was very sensitive to the site and could refine the house and return it to its classic modern roots.

I immediately thought of William Nicholas, a former colleague and friend who had worked in my studio. With his wife, Susan Budd, he has an architectural firm, Nicholas/Budd. Bill grew up in California and loved and understood the West Coast and its landscape, and he honed his plant and site knowledge while working for five years with my firm. He had long admired the modern architecture of Southern California, having grown up

Nicholas, we designed terraces adjacent to this living center of the house. The terrace facing the ocean has a roof that feels continuous with the ceiling of the main room. This covering tempers the glare of the southwestern sun. The terrace is furnished with one very low chair, so the view across the beach grass has a seamless connection with the ocean. The sensuous grass, always flirting with its pale feathers, is planted very close to the house's large glass windows. The house feels as if it is on a beach dune, when in fact it is on a cliff overlooking the beach.

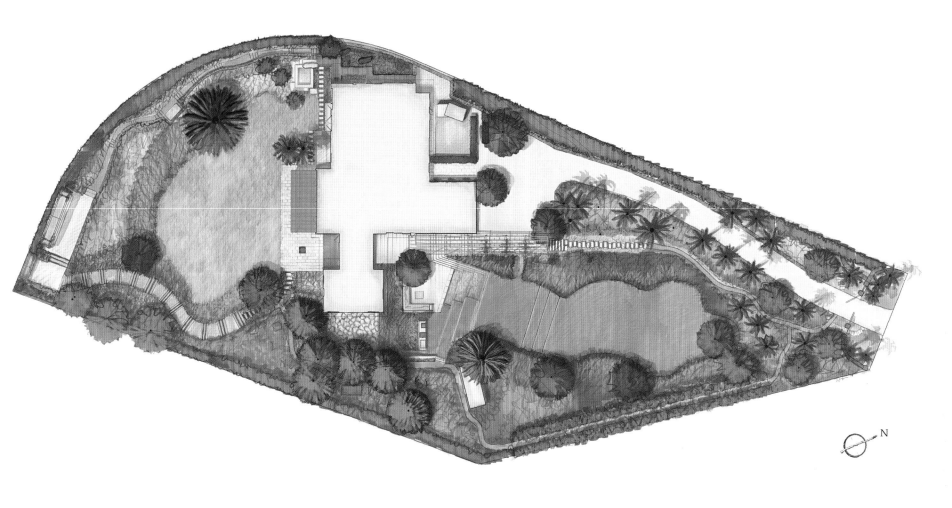

world, a dream-perfect beach house

Previous pages: *Stone risers across the lawn stripe the gentle rise of the garden and create broad grass steps.* Above: *Ground plan of the beachside site.* Left: *The big lawn before the redesign.*

A dramatic coral tree in the center of the east terrace provides shade and is sheltered from the ocean's wind by the guest pavilion. The tree anchors the long L-shaped stucco banquette to the space. With lots of softly hued pillows to lean on, the banquette makes a cozy place to talk. This living space has a table and chairs that can be easily rearranged and moved to the front south terrace on a beautiful hot late summer day or for an early fall lunch. The barbeque, placed in a stone wall behind the banquettes, has a sliver of a view to the ocean and ample room for a frisky fire's smoke to blow away from the sitting areas.

boundary and entrance from the motor court. This axial view goes straight through the owners' glass study, an inspirational place to work, to the ocean beyond. In the other direction a mysterious garden path winds behind the huge grass waves and intricate plantings of succulents—*Senecio mandraliscae*, aloes, aeoniums, and echeverias—and palms, contrasting with the simplicity of the lawn and the mass plantings of *Miscanthus transmorrisonensis*. The sacred trees of the Maori of New Zealand (*Metrosideros excelsus*) in the motor court soften the light in the court and shade the parked cars.

Lining the sides of the lawn, waves of giant grass blow in the ocean breeze

Imagine being able to dream and cook at the same time. Gentle water flows over shallow steps onto ribbons of stone that suggest tide pools, completing the side of the patio. It is nice to sit on the low steps and dangle one's toes in the water.

Behind this modern water piece, a soothing green lawn continues up the slight grade. It is intermittently slashed with shallow steps, continuing the strong axial tension to the corner, where another coral tree is planted. Lining the sides of the lawn are huge plantings of tall grass whose bent-over flowers suggest waves. The vista is mesmerizing and calming.

The natural entrance to the house is along the east garden. A wood pergola extends the strong axis and makes a pleasant

An outdoor room to the right of the front entrance is hedged with pittosporum (*Pittosporum crassifolium*), another good coastal plant. Behind the hedge is the owner's outdoor art studio with a kiln and potting wheel. Rekindling his early career, he works outside, as ceramicists have for thousands of years, no doubt influenced by the sound of the ocean, the beauty of the light, and the gentleness of the climate—a true paradise on the Pacific.

Broad steps continue under the trellis and cross the entire garden. The rusty plumes of the tall grass (Miscanthus sinensis) *dance next to you as you walk through the garden.*

Previous pages, left: *Joe Sturges,
from our design studio, designed
a water feature that evokes
local tide pools; shallow water
runs over beds with pieces of
ledger stone set on the diagonal.*
Previous pages, right: *A coral
tree* (Erythrina caffra) *shades
the terrace. The well-cushioned
long banquette makes a perfect
place for a nap or a chat.* Right:
*The little guesthouse hidden
under a Canary Island palm
underplanted with softly waving
grass offers a quiet retreat with a
porthole view of the ocean.*

Above: *Almost hiding
the house is a hillside of
Mexican feather grass,
"blond hair of the earth,"
as my friend John Greenlee
once called* Nassella
tenuissima. *Whenever I see
a planting of it, I envision
planted heads of California
surfer chicks.* Left: *House
under construction.*

Above: *When you brush against the large planting of California native sage* (Salvia clevelandii) *on both sides of the steps, the pungent scent fills the air. It is hard to imagine that this is where a thirsty crabgrass lawn, left, once was.*

Right: *You can see Santa Catalina Island from this tempting spa, which warms you up after swimming in the cold Pacific. If you get too toasty, you can cool off on the lizard rock.* Following pages: *A tropical paradise with Kentia palms in a separate garden room near the house has a very long pool with luxurious steps on one side, one of our trademarks.*

Doheny Garden

My garden practice has grown up with Libby Doheny. We started working together in the late eighties when she discovered my work at the Santa Monica restaurant formerly called Camelions, now Chez Mimi. This site, one of my first opportunities to design in the area, gave me the chance to combine my earlier profession, interior design, with my newfound one, garden design.

Libby hired me to make floral and flowerpot arrangements to garden—and then adjust the colors and shapes to create a harmonious picture everywhere one might look. The correct relationship between a house and its site are of supreme importance.

When I first arrived at the long, rambling, one-story house, built by Roland Coate in the late forties, it appeared to be enveloped by large azaleas that had grown over the bottom of the window frames all along the foundation. It looked to me as if the house was sinking into the earth, like the *Titanic* sinking into the ocean. I wanted to save the house, so I tore out all of the foundation plantings and brought gravel right up to the building, so that the house's architecture could be seen again as one piece, giving it more importance. We painted the house a warm Naples yellow with dark olive green trim, which made it feel more like a part of the landscape.

For the front entrance of a house, I always try

pretty up her front door and back terrace for a party. This was how my first assistant, Sally Paul, and I began a professional relationship with the Doheny family in the early days of my practice. Without a solid reputation, a young company has to do whatever it can to get a foot in the door. Little by little, a few pots at a time, we gained Libby's trust. She eventually rewarded us with the job of creating a master plan for the entire property. We have been implementing the plan and refining her garden ever since.

One of my jobs as a designer is to enhance the architecture of the house and to make sure it feels natural and appropriate. I look at the entire picture—the house's interior and exterior, and the existing

To cool the courtyard and soften the sun's strong glare, I added a grove of California sycamores (*Platanus racemosa*) to the motor court. With their soft mottled gray, pale sepia, and burnt umber trunks and generous open leaves, the sycamores cast long, dappled shadows, serving as living columns for the house. The front entrance of a house, like the front hall on the inside, is the first experience one has upon arrival, and I always try to achieve a mood of hospitality and welcome in this vital space.

Libby loves to celebrate the seasons, and her demilune brick front steps make a perfect stage to greet visitors with flowerpots full of seasonal delights: pumpkins and orange and yellow autumnal

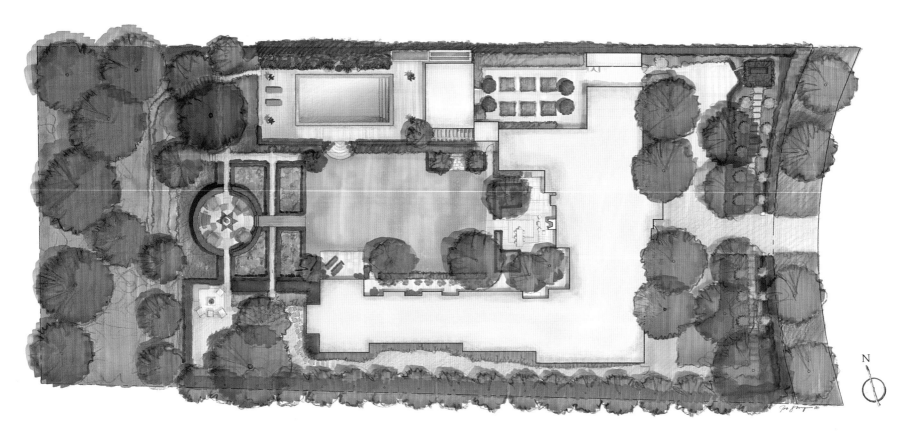

to achieve a mood of hospitality and welcome

plants, cyclamen and narcissus for the Christmas season, tulips and cymbidiums in the spring, cool-colored foliage and long-blooming flowers like blue hydrangea in the summer. The large British racing green leaves of sasanqua camellias fill the terra-cotta pots on the top porch landing. In bloom from December through March, they make a calm background for the showy pots on the steps year-round.

Inside the entrance on either side of the gate parallel to the house are two stone walks bordered by clipped, ball-shaped pittosporums (*Pittosporum crassifolium* 'Compacta') that help organize the adjacent beds. The beds would look messy without the axial balls, as they run

Previous pages: Wheels make a crunchy sound on the coarse gravel of the entrance court, announcing the arrival of visitors to the cheerful Naples yellow house. Above: The ground plan shows the quite formal structure of the property, but abundant plantings soften the orthogonal design of the many garden rooms.

rampant with perennials, shrub roses, and woody plants. It is the contrast of ordered form and exuberant growth that perks up these borders. Orange trees frame the edge of the motor court, scenting the air with their fragrant blossoms.

Beside the front corners of the house we put matching teak gates that open to the back of the house: The one on the south side leads to a private garden off the master bedroom, and the one on the north side leads to an organized service yard and vegetable garden. We make all of our gates out of teak. Recycled teak is readily available, and, if a gate is correctly built and installed using high-quality hardware, it will last forever, requiring little maintenance. My preference is to use Cabot stain in driftwood gray, lightly rubbed into the wood, which will take the new teak's redwood color down to a softer, more harmonious color in the landscape. Teak gates also look lovely if left to turn gray naturally, but it does take longer.

A number of years ago I fell in love with a kitchen garden in France that was shown in a shelter magazine. The garden was made up of rectangles approximately five by eight feet, each surrounded by a ten-inch-high stone border with gravel paths all around. Not only did I find this a tidy solution, but the size proved to be very practical, since one could reach the vegetables and fruits easily on both sides. Most of the vegetable gardens I have designed take this form.

A wooden pergola covered in pale blue trumpet flowers (*Thunbergia grandiflora*) shields the yard next to Libby's garden shed, its storage shelves filled with stacked pots and resting plants. Clearly, the shed is no rustic lean-to. Inside, Libby keeps her copy of the Sunset *Western Garden Book*, the local gardener's bible, which is dog-eared and notated like a telephone book. It is a practical item—not precious—because she uses it all of the time, dirty hands or not. Libby also refers to other books and seasonal catalogs to find dahlias, one of her specialty flowers, spring bulbs, and seeds. All of these, along

Clipped pittosporum balls tame the exuberantly planted borders of roses, perennials, and woody plants on both sides of the front gate. Without these orderly accents, the borders might seem messy and unkempt.

with special tools, straw hats, and boots, she keeps here next to her desk, which, through a charming window, overlooks the vegetable garden. This is Libby's special place to dream and plan additions and changes to her garden, as well as to pot up new plants or start seedlings. Her collection of old watering cans next to the front door adds a rustic touch. They are ready to be used as soon as a plant looks thirsty.

The Doheny garden faces west and has a grand view of the Santa Monica Mountains with a big lawn. When I first studied the site, the view was obscured by an overgrown magnolia (*Magnolia grandiflora*)

and birches that blocked the view. To remove a tree is a difficult and tremendous decision for everyone—me and my clients alike. But the spectacular view of the mountains, with colors constantly changing throughout the day and culminating in spectacular sunsets every evening, was much more exciting. So the tree came out. With careful

Previous pages: The view to the Santa Monica Mountains across the lawn from the terrace. Above: Hydrangea 'Endless Summer' lives up to its name from late spring on. Opposite: Periwinkle trumpets of the jacaranda weep petal tears on the lawn in late spring.

pruning I opened up the other trees in what I call "making windows" to allow a beautiful view through them—blue sky peeking through green leaves, with alluring silhouettes formed by the foreground trees at the end of the day.

We extended the terrace adjoining the house for dining alfresco. We planted sycamores here, too, to provide shade from the brutal western sun and to link the front and back of the house visually, always one of my favorite design ideas. We moved a barbeque away from the center of this outdoor room and replaced it with a fireplace, refocusing the space into a place to converse, lounge, relax, and eat. Granny Doheny's comfortable old furniture was re-covered in soft shades of green, and soon this space took on an additional function, becoming Will Doheny's outdoor living room for cigar smoking with the boys. A closet for Will's portable television made this his favorite spot to spend most evenings.

I have always admired the way Harold Nicholson and Vita Sackville-West laid out Sissinghurst, their garden in Kent, England. Harold designed the architectural bones of the gardens, and Vita filled them in. I think I have a little more of Harold, the architect, as I really like to design the bones best. From Sissinghurst, I have borrowed the conifer roundel, or rounded hedge, for the end of the garden. Instead of the yew (*Taxus baccata*) used at Sissinghurst, I planted five-gallon Italian cypress (*Cupressus sempervirens*), which are more successful when planted small. By keeping them clipped to six feet in height, we have allowed these trees to grow robust within five years.

The roundel's center has a hexagonal stone fountain with red stone diamond-shaped inlays and a raised bowl on a pedestal. The splashing and cascading water can be seen from the terrace, uniting the space and enticing one to explore further into the space which is encircled by tangerine and lemon trees.

Graceful semicircular steps with potted succulents along both sides lead up to the swimming pool and the Balinese pavilion, which Libby added after a trip to Bali. We added flowering trees, to give the site a different color for every season. In late winter, the bluish white flowers of almond trees welcome the spring.

Left: *The once hot and glary terrace.* Opposite: *Now sheltered by sycamores, the terrace has acquired a new fireplace, and the barbeque has been moved to the side closer to the kitchen. Will Doheny spends many evenings in front of the new fireplace, bringing a television outside as soon as spring brings warmer nights.*

In mid-spring, the delicate yellow flowers of the slightly twisted small golden trumpet tree (*Tabebuia chrysotricha*) bloom. These are followed by the late spring–early summer show of the jacaranda (*Jacandra mimosifolia*) from Brazil, whose periwinkle blooms are vibrant against the gray of Southern California's "June gloom" fog. By mid-summer, huge egg-yolk-colored floral medallions of senna (*Cassia leptophylla*) cover the front of the Balinese pavilion, reflecting in the pool as the sun sets. Another senna (*Cassia alata*), a smaller member of the cassia family with pale Naples yellow

flowers, blooms through the fall. The huge red fruits of the Chinese persimmon (*Diospyros kaki*) are the essence of autumn color, and they complete the flowering cycle.

It was vital that the flowers enhance the colors of the house. When choosing this collection of trees, Libby and I took great care to make sure that colors created a harmonious palette. We did have one exception—an old, twisted crape myrtle (*Lagerstroemia indica*) with bright mauve-pink flowers. While I didn't care for the color of the flowers against the house, the trunk's color and character

were so striking during the rest of the year, looking particularly sculptural during the winter, that it had to stay.

Libby has kept us involved with the garden, and we have honed and refined the design over many years. She knows that good housekeeping is the main reason her garden is so successful; she respects her gardeners' talents and knows they need to continuously tend the garden to maintain her high standards. Libby's garden is one of her life's achievements, which enhances our design and makes our work with her a delight.

Opposite: *Skilled artisan José Aguirre and Linda Jassim from my studio designed and built a stone fountain with inlaid panels of terra-cotta and pink sandstone. Four lemon trees are set in beds cut into the terrace at the center of the Italian cypress roundel.*
Above: *Roses gathered from the garden fill the house from April through December.*

Right: *Yolk-yellow flowers of* Cassia leptophylla *reflected in the pool. Libby Doheny added the romantic Balinese-style pool house after a trip to Bali. Above: José Aguirre built a wall fountain designed by our studio, using shards of stone to make panels flanking a carved antique Balinese one. Following pages: Colorful plant details enliven the Doheny garden.*

Faring House Garden

Lauren and Richard King purchased a property in Los Angeles, which they named Faring House, that had belonged to Fanny Brice, a legendary star made even more famous by Barbra Streisand's portrayal of her in *Funny Girl*. It was a solid brick house built in the twenties and surrounded by several acres of grounds. The Kings liked the location, but they felt that the house needed to be brought up to current standards, and they wanted a more traditional East Coast style garden, no bougainvillea and no birds of paradise. They hired me to do the landscape and I suggested the rest of the team: Oscar Shamamian, a renowned New York architect and partner

and its grounds together very carefully. I was able to contribute some of my early experiences as an interior designer to the project by working closely with the Kings and their architect, suggesting terraces and porches.

Lauren had culled photographs from magazines and books of her favorite rooms and gardens, a terrific aid for me as her designer as I was quickly able to see her preferences. She loved the green gardens of New England, some with ordered clipped boxwood, others parklike with lots of big deciduous trees and a background of dark evergreens. She returned over and over to a house and garden in Connecticut that was set at the edge of a wood with a grand vista overlooking the neighboring countryside, which changed with the seasons. Long allées of deciduous trees in the French style framed the view.

The swimming pool and flower gardens were carefully set to the left side of the vista and enclosed with hedges forming garden rooms. I think it was the serenity of the site that appealed to her. It kept the messy outdoor activities in their own place, which in

The views from the house and its adjoining terrace and

in Murray and Shamamian, known for classical designs; and Peter McCoy, the best local contractor, known for fastidious attention to detail and ability to handle large high-end residential projects.

What started out as a remodeling project segued into a complete redesign of the property, what we call in the field "scope creep." The architecture of the house became much grander, and all of the spaces adjoining the house had to be redesigned. By assembling the project team at the beginning of the project, we were able to knit the house

this northern climate was not used for three seasons. I actually had visited this house and its gardens in Connecticut several times, and knew what she wanted, so I liberally adapted some of its concepts for her house near Beverly Hills.

To achieve the parklike serenity, I decided that the views from the house and its adjoining terrace and porches would be mainly lawn and trees and we would tuck the now traditional California activities into outdoor rooms. We concluded that the existing very

porches were planned to have a broad, parklike quality

large sycamores on the west side of the property felt good with the house and would become the dominant species on the site. We started by moving several of them to make room for the swimming pool and new pool house. Sycamores move easily and also grow quickly. With an allée added along the new driveway, they surrounded the house on both sides. The house was now set in a grove of sycamores that shaded the big terrace and softened the light coming into the house during the long sunny Southern California seasons.

Previous pages: *The stately house with its generous bluestone stairs and elegant stone pots comes slowly into view from the gently curving new drive to the motor court. Above: The ground plan shows the big lawn at the center of the landscape surrounded by garden rooms for a variety of outdoor activities.*

Brilliant colorist Scott Flax used the subtle colors of the sycamore bark as his inspiration for the house colors. Painting the red brick a creamy white and the shutters a taupe gray, he visually quieted the house down and settled it as part of the grove. In winter the bare trees become stately columns to the house and allow the beautiful slanted winter sun into the south-facing rooms.

The old-fashioned porch with pale robin's egg ceiling overlooks a koi pond framed by tall hedges of western red cedar (*Thuja plicata*). Knowing that curiosity sometimes gets the best of puppies and children, I like to put a ledge step just below the surface of the water, so that if they fall in they'll have something to climb up on.

Within the pond the water plants are planted in concrete containers, with terra-cotta roof tiles beneath them. The roof tiles are piled up like a honeycomb, making apartment houses for the fish to hide and lay eggs in. This also helps keep the koi safe when there is a marauding heron, raccoon, or cat messing about the pond looking for dinner. I saw tiles used this way in the fish ponds at Pompeii, and liked the simple solution.

This porch has become Mr. King's favorite room: no surprise as this was one of his special requests. It adjoins the family room and is not too far from the kitchen, which means it is used all the time. With comfortable furniture from Treillage, Bunny Williams' shop in New York, it even has an armoire with a television set and a fireplace for cool evenings. A dining table for family lunches and suppers is set up ready to go.

From the very beginning Mr. and Mrs. King have taken a great interest in the grounds and gardens of Faring House. I have observed that, like most men, Richard adores lots of lawn, a good view, and his trees. Lauren loves flowers and the details of the garden, which she continues to add to and develop; this past year, she added an organic vegetable garden.

Right: *A new grove of sycamores softens the light coming onto the terrace and into the house during the long sunny Southern California dry seasons.* Left: *The dining room window and terrace before the new gardens were designed.*

The guesthouse with new garden plantings (above) and as it appeared before (left). Opposite: *White heliotrope with the old-fashioned scent of Good & Plenty candy along the path to the pool garden.*

Above: *Faring House,
embellished with inviting
new terraces and a covered
porch with rocking chairs.*
Left: *The house before the
redesign.* Opposite: *The
koi pond is framed by tall
hedges of western red cedar
(Thuja plicata).*

Water plants grow in concrete containers,
with terra-cotta roof tiles beneath them,
making apartment houses for the fish to
hide and lay eggs in. I saw such a use of
tiles at Pompeii, and liked the solution

Above: *A stylish new pool house by New York architect Oscar Shamamian.* Left: *The old view across the lawn.* Opposite: *A jacaranda tree blooming during what is locally called "June gloom," when the Pacific marine fog comes in and anything purple glows in the soft light.*

Below: *The original pool complex. Right:*
The new pool house, based on an old carriage
house, displays a standing seam roof and
a charming cupola. The purple haze of a
Brazilian jacaranda lights up the terrace.

Beverly Canon Gardens

Designing the first park in the center of Beverly Hills, celebrated for its illustrious shopping district locally known as the golden triangle, was a thrilling but often daunting task. Building a garden on top of a parking structure is not easy, not to mention the high visibility such a park might have. It might even become a destination like Paley Park in New York. Beverly Hills is so glamorous: a mecca for Hollywood's rich and famous, the home to our country's film royalty, and a fantasy place to so many people.

I thought about all my travels and many of the parks I have visited: what I enjoyed and, as important, what I did and did not find comfortable, particularly in countries with a climate similar to ours. I have lived in New York, Florence, and Rome, so I had first-hand experience in these older cities.

The space, 311 feet long, connects two streets, and lies between a new luxury hotel, the Beverly Hills Montage, and a narrow garden building, which has restaurants and cafés. Both have arcades the length of the garden, immediately giving the area a reference to the past. I feel it is one of most attractive, intimate, and comfortable ancient building types for both town and country. The architects for the hotel, Hill Glazier, had drawn on earlier California architecture to interpret this classical tradition, which in turn came from ancient vernacular architecture around the Mediterranean.

For me good small public spaces have several basic qualities: a nice place to sit with moveable chairs, a canopy overhead provided by trees or umbrellas, protection from the wind, and fountains. These amenities can be enhanced with the addition of a café, plants, and flowers. If larger, the park will have flexible spaces, a lawn for children and small events, places to sit in the sun or out of the sun, proximity to shopping and street life.

We divided the park into five orthogonal courtyards of varying sizes. Formal clipped hedges surround all of these spaces except the lawn. Clipped pyramidal conifers punctuate entrances to the spaces and add vertical interest; soft plantings of miniature olive trees, germander (*Teucrium fruiticans*), and westringia (*Westringia rosmariniformis*) in grays and greens complement the dark greens. The central courtyard has a somewhat grand splashy fountain, which draws you into the middle of the gardens. Columnar magnolias (*Magnolia grandiflora* 'Blanchard') planted in each of its four corners and large terra-cotta pots filled with citrus give the feeling of an Italian private garden.

Coming from busy Beverly Drive one takes several steps down into a sunken garden court set up with tables and chairs—modern steel colored versions of classic French park chairs—for visitors to bring their own lunches, have a coffee from the nearby café or bakery of Thomas Keller (of French Laundry fame), play chess, write a letter, have a little quiet time, or rest from shopping. Four tipu trees (*Tipuana tipu*) of the pea family with pale apricot to creamy yellow flowers create dappled light over some of the tables. When it's very

Previous pages: *The park's central courtyard looking toward the Beverly Hills Montage Hotel.* Opposite: *Places to sit with or without tables encourage visitors to stay. Next to the agave fountain the air is fragrant from the blossoms of a potted lemon tree.*

sunny, umbrellas will be brought out to shade the remaining tables. Gently trickling water from a shallow bowl near the top of a small stone fountain flows over the edge and into the basin, calming the nerves and lightly masking the sounds of the city.

The simple limestone pavers used throughout the park and in the arcades frame the edge of this courtyard garden and surround the tree pits. Softly colored tiny pebbles set in pale ochre concrete appear to form a gravel terrace and blend with the limestone edging and fountain. A stone mosaic lines the fountain basin in warm Roman colors with a simple pattern in the Greco-Roman tradition.

In the other three patio spaces, these colors are repeated as terra-cotta carpets within the limestone paving. Most distinctive are the sparkling Persian blue mosaics in the center fountain, a color I fell in love with on a trip to Iran. Echoing the sky and water, this blue is a reminder of the preciousness of water in our climate, the water that brings life and coolness to the environment.

When you walk south on Canon Drive on the east side of the garden, near the entrance to the hotel, you hear the sound of water, but its source is mysterious. The intriguing sounds invite you to discover this garden oasis, perhaps to sit on the limestone step benches around the lawn, or to pull a chair close to long wall fountains reminiscent of those at Villa d'Este near Rome and put your feet up, savoring the coolness and energy from the flowing water. The Mexican sycamores around the lawn, bare in winter, allow a little welcome sun. The big leaves come out in spring, providing shade during the long, hot dry season.

Opposite: *I believe in making intimate outdoor spaces within a large park with moveable tables and chairs where people can shift their seats according to the weather. The lawn, shown on the plan,* right, *is used for play or for special events.*

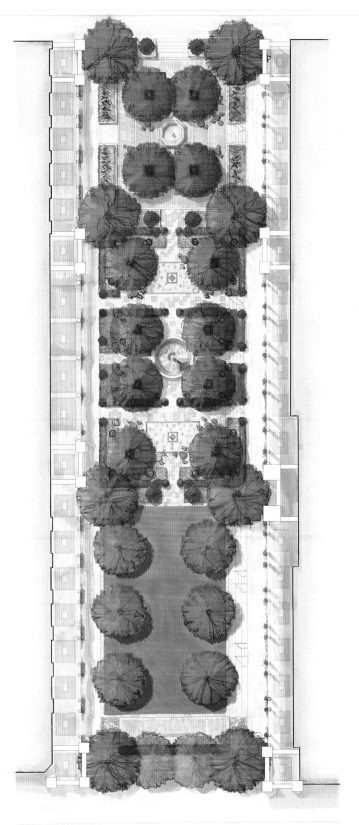

Ganz Garden

Collaborating with Jo Ann and Julian Ganz was a stimulating experience in every way. They are sophisticated, well traveled, and have discerning taste, challenging me in my choices and ideas. We had long, thought-provoking conversations about art, design, history, style, and function. We all agreed that their new garden needed to relate better to the house and its surroundings, should be simple and serene, and should be more appropriate to their current lifestyle. With their children grown up, they could refine the garden to be in keeping with their less hectic life.

Alfred T. "Hap" Gilman designed their classic modern house, was a classic modern L-shaped mid-century, and so I designed the garden my mother had always wanted.

Mother had contacted Thomas Church, California's most prominent landscape architect, to design a garden for our new house in southern Delaware but was unable to persuade him to come. She had always been interested in Japanese gardens and had wanted a garden in this style. We had several books on the gardens of Kyoto in our library. The two of us often looked at the pictures together and talked about what we would borrow from them and how we would design our garden. Her taste was very simple and unpretentious; she thought that rocks could not possibly be appropriate in our tidewater landscape—they would be too Disneyland, in the same category as stone dwarfs and flamingos. We both adored the ponds, anything asymmetrical, dramatically shaped pine trees, and of course iris. My design sensibility was definitely formed at home.

The first project at the Ganz house was the courtyard and

The motor court is planted with four dark green

which was part of the former Phipps estate. It was built in 1962 and their landscape architect was the renowned Edward Huntsman-Trout—a strong design team. It was a little daunting to follow Huntsman-Trout, but I got up my courage and plunged in. The house was so similar to the one my parents had built in the early fifties that I felt right at home. As an artistic child, I had designed and redesigned my parents' house and gardens a million ways, often with my mother. Deep down in my psyche I had already formed the background for this garden. The Ganzes' house, like my parents', swimming pool. To me there was too much concrete hardscape, which in the bright sun was full of heat and glare. We all agreed it was not as inviting as it could be. The handsome aggregate concrete was laid out in squares with thin wooden lines separating them. Influenced by a Mondrian painting, I remade the grid in a different pattern, taking out several squares and turning them into planted green rectangles and a long rectangular koi pond. I planted the foreground next to the house with three twisted black pines and mounds of clipped African boxwood (*Myrsine africana*). Now you

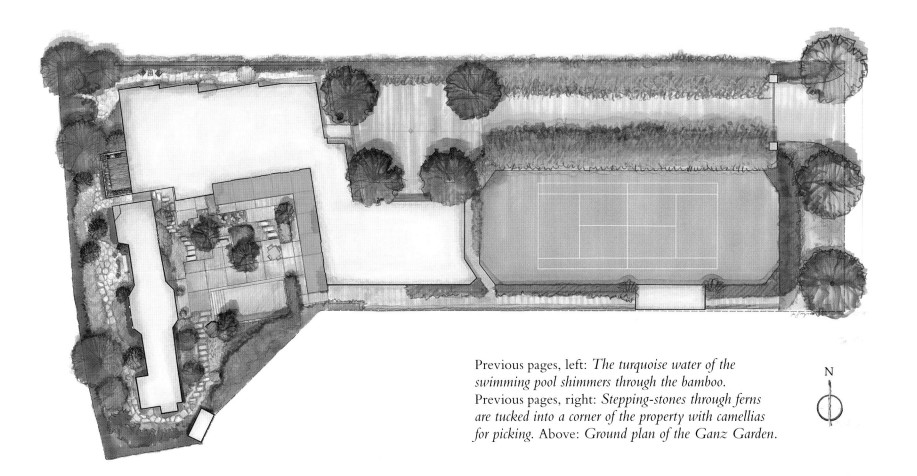

Previous pages, left: *The turquoise water of the swimming pool shimmers through the bamboo.* Previous pages, right: *Stepping-stones through ferns are tucked into a corner of the property with camellias for picking.* Above: *Ground plan of the Ganz Garden.*

N

stone pines providing cool shade and a lovely sound

viewed the garden from under a conifer parasol across undulating miniature mountains with a stream of 'Grandma's Purple Flag' iris running next to the mountains—all traditional elements borrowed from Japanese paintings of gardens.

This small garden veiled the view of the concrete terrace from the house, with just a glimpse of the sparkling water of the swimming pool. By repeating some of the same plants on the opposite side of the pool, the garden was visually united and made to seem larger. Small slightly enclosed spaces within the plantings became seating areas, one for a bench for contemplation or for holding your towel while you were swimming, the other for dining. Defining these spaces and breaking up the sea of concrete enlarged the space and helped control the sun's glare.

Huntsman-Trout had placed a large pale ledge stone next to the pool with a tiny waterfall, which we adjusted to a gentle trickle. The movement of the large koi in their new pond, the flittering of small birds around the bird feeder, and the deep coo of doves under the planter added gentle natural life to the garden.

The entrance to the house was our next project. A strange grotto filled with dank water ran inside to an atrium garden. Atrium gardens are often dark, making it difficult to grow plants, and this one was no exception. We were always trying new plants with little success: so discouraging. We dismantled this water feature and liberated the koi to their new sunny pond, with fresh running water and aquatic plants. Now they were the center of attention, and from all of the rooms surrounding the courtyards one could catch flickers of silver, gold, and Chinese red. They were so tantalizing that they became pets, and enjoyed being fed from the hand. The atrium was paved with the limestone of the adjoining dining room and a handsome birdbath was planted with hardy easy succulents. No more trying to make fish and plants happy.

We replaced old hedges with giant timber bamboo on either side of the driveway, making it a tunnel. The motor court was planted with four dark green stone pines (*Pinus pinea*), providing cool shade and a lovely sound. One of the pines, placed in front of the car park, cast a dark shade that obscured the black cars. The entrance became more mysterious and elegant.

I think the drastic change in the courtyard and the Ganzes'

enjoyment of the process influenced them to refine the interior and exterior of the house. They hired Philip Oates, a French interior designer now living in Los Angeles, who understood both their sophistication and the architecture of the house. His approach was just what the house needed to make it into a glamorous contemporary masterpiece. Together, we analyzed and refined every aspect of the exterior, using theatrical tricks like putting mirrors on the roof to cover up unsightly ducts and reflect the bamboo and pine trees instead. We had a lot of fun solving complicated design issues and shared an intuitive response to what needed to be changed to strengthen and enhance the look of the house.

Oates softened the interior by changing the wood color to a soft gray and using materials that looked harmonious with the outdoors. I made new gardens, repeating the palette of the pines and bamboo on both sides of the house, setting the entire house in the middle of a garden.

This garden continues to be loved and cared for; the Ganzes are willing to provide the funds to keep the integrity of the design and the health of the plants at an optimum level. Their love of their garden is the best present they can give me.

Far left: *A straight dull path became a small seating place.* Left: *The former hot and glary drive into the Ganz property.* Opposite: *Giant timber bamboo is in the process of forming an arched cathedral ceiling over the drive.*

Like my parents' house, the Ganzes' was mid-century

Opposite: *An Italian stone pine, one of four, with its boughs draped over the front door, and a low planting of shore juniper creeping around the sculpture.* Above: *A stepping-stone path.* Following pages, left: *A wall of the enclosed garden is shrouded in chartreuse-veined chocolate creeper,* Parthenocissus henryana. *Following pages, right: In the early morning, plum trees shade a tiny terrace of stepping-stones with 'Elfin' thyme between them.*

modern, so I felt right at home designing here

Above: *A secluded terrace for reflection next to the library.*
Right: *The Venetian-plaster walled garden with a teak deck.*
Japanese maples change color, marking the changing seasons.
The Ganz gardener puts camellias in the small container that
fills with gently dripping water from a copper spout.

Above: *Myrsine clipped to resemble mountains backed by gnarled black pines frames the view from the house, shields it from the southern light, and breaks up the formerly huge concrete terrace.*
Opposite: *Creeping wooly thyme softens rectilinear stepping-stones.*

Previous pages: *Languid koi are mesmerizing with their flickering colors of orange, gold, and silver in the dark water.* Above: *Black pines are repeated next to the swimming pool, echoing those near the house.* Opposite: *Under the overhanging pine a lizard rock with a tiny water source that trickles into the pool is a cool place to sit with your toes in the water on a hot day.*

Martin-Sykes Garden

It is very rewarding to still be involved with a garden that was built from scratch almost twenty years ago. The structure of this garden, its large trees and shrubs, has finally reached the size that I had envisioned. The scale has slowly changed the feeling of the garden. When it was first planted, the garden felt sunny, often too hot, open and exposed, similar to the adjacent native chaparral in the Santa Monica hills and visible to all of the houses in the neighborhood. Over the years, the garden has become enclosed, more mysterious, cooler, and shadier.

Gene and Tracy Sykes, the new owners, worked with the original architect, Richard "Dick" Martin, to expand the house to accommodate their family of four children by acquiring the property above them. Dick and I had designed the original gardens together and my firm continues to oversee new plantings and to hone and refine the old garden.

We planted the east and south boundaries with fast-growing black acacias (*Acacia melanoxylon*), and they have done their job, blocking out the roofs of adjacent properties. We planted small coast live oaks parallel to the house and in the middle of the garden. They are now large, and their majestic presence adds dappled shade over the paths, foreground screening, and depth to the garden. The native oak grows quite fast for the first twenty-five years of its life, then it slows down and its form becomes broader and more interesting, turning gnarled with age. I consider these oaks the elder grandfathers of the western cultural landscape and they are quite sacred to Native Americans. We lost one of the original plantings because its trunk had been partly covered with dirt and mulch. Oaks are particularly sensitive to too much water and trunk rot, more than most trees. It is very important to check around all trees when and after they are planted to make sure the connection of the trunk to the root is exposed.

The long axial stone stairs are softened with wooly thyme growing in between its crevices and by the curves of the mounding landscape. In the heat of the day the thyme's pungent fragrance distracts one from the steepness of the site. The stairs lead to the bottom of the property and connect with paths woven along the contours of the land.

To the left the path leads to a magical grove of adolescent blue gum saplings, seedlings of the huge eucalyptus (*Eucalyptus globulus*) that dominates the top of the garden. Planted with many gray foliage plants and a soft native bunch grass, this magical place is augmented by the sculptural furniture of Claude Lalanne. I am quite sure that fairies come out and dance here in the Moon Garden. One midsummer's night a chamber group played for a group of us at dusk, and at another time for a garden party.

One of our major jobs as garden designers is to "fix" or enhance the views, blocking unsightly houses, telephone poles, and anything that distracts from or stands in the way of connecting the garden to the local natural environment, the sky, the ocean, and the protected Santa Monica Mountains. Connecting the views also helps define the garden, ensures privacy, and usually makes the property feel bigger because it has captured "borrowed landscape."

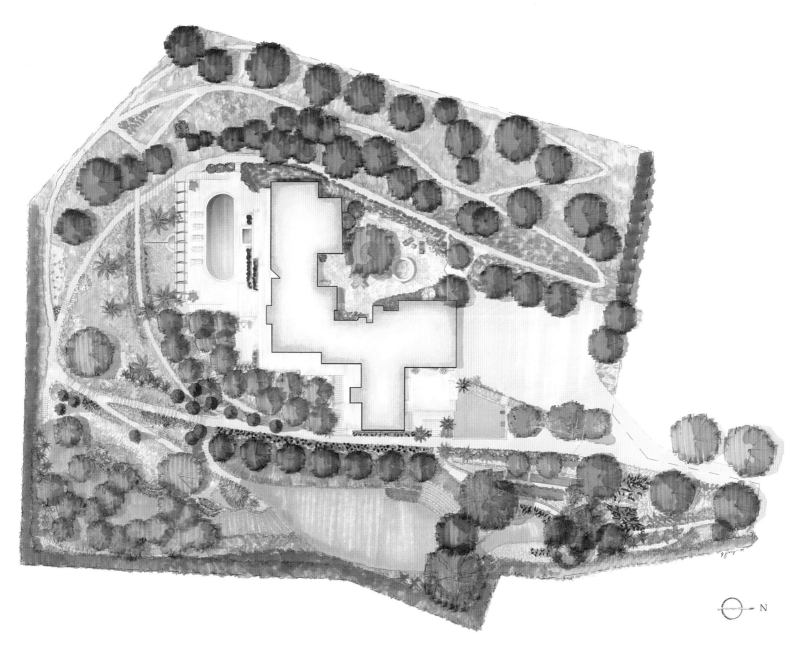

N

Previous pages: *Ginkgo-leaf furniture by French artists Claude and François-Xavier Lalanne in the eucalyptus grove's native meadow grass.*
Left: *Before the redesign, the steep hillside revealed neighbors' roofs below.*
Above: *Ground plan shows how winding paths follow the hillside's contours.*

One of my favorite axioms is "the more you define the space, the larger it becomes."

At the top of the hill and below the swimming pool we planted my favorite periwinkle blue iris (*Iris x germanica* 'Breakers') along a path. I love to plant them as if they form a stream and have done this many times. I think I must have seen a photograph in one of my mother's garden books years ago of a Japanese garden with iris winding though a meadow. Here they run through the shimmering silver of the olive grove and through the grove's underplanted carpet of rosemary, which repeats the periwinkle blue of the iris in its tiny flowers.

Olives make a good neutral background, setting off the sunny Mediterranean-climate border of brightly flowered plants below: orange lion's tail (*Leonotis leonurus*), egg-yolk perennial marigold (*Tagetes lemmoni*), Jerusalem sage with yellow flowers on wooly gray foliage (*Phlomis fruiticosa*), many salvias, large chartreuse globes of euphorbia (*Euphorbia characias wulfenii*), and giant blue spires of Pride of Madeira (*Echium candicans*), which have seeded throughout the border and southern part of the garden.

Italian cypresses we planted fifteen years ago have become gigantic dark olive green obelisks scattered throughout the garden casting long shadows—quite formidable at dusk, scattering the little children when they play hide and seek in the garden.

With the renovation and additions to the house, we added an amphitheater and broad new steps carved out of the steep hillside to connect to a flat playing field for the children. We replaced precarious broken concrete stairs with sweetwater stone, one of my favorite sandstones because it goes so well with our indigenous soil colors. The sitting steps of the amphitheater are a good place to watch a game of tag or soccer, and perhaps dress-up plays and future family events. The walls of the amphitheater are wavy pink purple curtains of a large grass (*Muhlenbergia capillaris*) and blonde native deer grass (*Muhlenbergia rigens*).

A small amphitheater softened by purple muhly grass backed by a curtain of Miscanthus, *where family and friends can watch the children frolicking or performing on the lawn from broad sitting steps of sweetwater stone, a favorite sandstone in our studio.*

Above the playing field is a stand of grand blue gums (*Eucalpytus globulus*) and a tropical-style garden. Using big-leaved plants like fatsia (*Fatsia japonica*) and giant birds of paradise (*Strelitzia nicolai*), dorycnium (*Dorycnium hirsutum*), several gingers, and a ficus with fat juicy leaves (*Ficus auriculata*) makes this jungle another good place for hide and seek. The dark stately trees have changed the garden's light and the climate.

I have fond memories of coming over after work to the Martins' to share a bottle of wine and wander around the land and design with Dick. As we walked about, we would discuss plant ideas and combinations. I would suggest something and he would veto it; then I would try another and he would veto it with some

from the list, refining, refining, refining. Gathering one of each of the plants that you have picked, bringing them to the site, and editing after you see where they are to go is probably the best way to design, though a tad indulgent. This intuitive, tactile, and organic approach is much scorned by many professionals, but this is exactly where my real skills as an artist flourish. Our art is three-dimensional and I have yet to see a way of designing on paper in the studio that is nearly as successful. I imagine the space and pick a palette of plants, but sometimes on site the light isn't right, there is a tree or shrub in the distance that you want to connect to, the combinations are unpredictable, or some small thing needs to be brought out and celebrated. There are always surprises, and even

Designing on site, using plant lists, is usually the best way to get good results

kind of cryptic remark like, "It will look like a Chinese dinner," meaning too many colors or plants with no structure. I didn't give up, though I often wanted to throw the glass of wine at him. (I just didn't want to waste the wine, as he always served the best. In fact, he has gone on to become a vineyard owner, producing a top-notch wine called Versant.) His quest for some imaginary perfection paid off, though, and his demands were very good for me. I refined my plant choices and became even more aware of the structure, texture, and colors of the plants.

In many ways, designing on site, particularly creating the planting plans, is the best way to get good results. Have a great list of plants that you know, take it to the site with you, and pick

with photographs one can't capture every subtlety.

I remember a quite successful landscape architect saying to me that she only came to the site once, and did all of the drawings, both hardscape and plant plans, in her office. I knew she really wanted to be an architect and that plants were very minor, probably a nuisance to her, as they are alive and unpredictable, which is of course why I like designing with plants!

A serpentine broken concrete wall built by Luis Munoz forms a pedestal for a magnificent agave (Agave americana) set off by a bed of dark phormium and surrounded by pale blue-gray senecio (Senecio mandraliscae).

Above: *Strong axial stairs of sweetwater stone cross through the winding paths on the hill. Tough Mediterranean plants line the walk. Bronze cannas, several salvias, Leucadendron 'Safari Sunset', and phormium grow next to robust Italian cypress.*
Opposite: *The tropical garden's giant birds of paradise, tree ferns, euphorbias, and Agave attenuata are good-looking in both tropical and Mediterranean settings.*

Norton Simon Sculpture Garden

The Norton Simon was my first public garden. One of my goals in my work has been to receive recognition in the private sector for my garden design so that I would be asked to do public gardens. I have always felt that there are not enough gardens that can be enjoyed by everyone. Also, I have always been fascinated with utopian ideas. In my teens I was fixated on utopian novels, and earlier, in the third grade, I read thirty-five biographies of famous people who had worked to make the world a better place, so I think my idealism and desire to make things beautiful started very early.

In 1995 I was asked by Frank Gehry and Jennifer Jones

wanted a comparable garden. The building had been the Pasadena Art Museum and had housed contemporary art, so it was not appropriate for a collection of Old Masters, fine nineteenth-century Impressionists, and early twentieth-century modernist paintings with strong bronze sculptures in the garden.

What a dilemma: how to relate the damp of temperate central France to the dry heat of Mediterranean-like California? Monet's exuberant, almost abstract flower paintings came to mind—the water lilies, the peonies, nasturtiums, the iris, and of course the mutable water. I have been to Giverny several times and the garden has a wild, out-of-control feeling with no obvious plan, much like the paintings. The pond with its famous green bridge and weeping willows was the most memorable feature. Exuberant plantings covered the paths, climbed walls and trellises, and cascaded into the pond. There was no place to sit and no place to rest your eyes from this riot of color, but there were masses of flowers to paint. I could picture Monet setting up his easel among the nasturtiums.

Mrs. Simon said in her deep dramatic voice,

Simon, the famous Hollywood actress, to design a new garden for the Norton Simon Museum. Frank's description of what he wanted was to "cover up the building and don't fuck it up." Mrs. Simon had recently been to Giverny and she told me in her deep dramatic voice, "Nancy darling, I want a garden just like Claude Monet's Giverny."

She talked about how she wanted the garden to relate to the great painting collection in the museum. Gehry was remodeling the interior of the museum to better suit the collection and she

I had enjoyed the fullness, the overblown masses of color, and the sheer abundance, and I loved the murky pond with water lilies. It touched down deep into my Tidewater memories of messing about in ponds, marshes, and creeks. As a child I had the freedom to wander all over the place as long as I was home in time for dinner. Water lilies and bald cypresses in the ponds have always been my favorites, so mysterious and mesmerizing. I could float in a canoe or lie on a dock and watch the life of mammals, reptiles, insects, and plants around the water and daydream for hours on

N

"Nancy, I want a garden just like Monet's Giverny"

end. When creating gardens, I have noticed that often we want to have what we remember from our childhood—a favorite tree, flowers, or a special place.

Taking out the long rectilinear pond in the center of the Norton Simon garden was my boldest move. I felt a naturally formed pond would be more dramatic and romantic, and it was also my strongest memory from both Giverny and from home. I was worried about the shape as so many little naturally shaped ponds do not look as if they belong where they are. They just look hokey,

with little wishing wells and shorelines rimmed in river rocks of all the same size: no beach, no boggy plants, and no mystery. I went to my large atlas and traced lakes from all over the world and came up with the right shape. I wanted the pond to go around the corner of the building, so it would lead you to discover more sculpture tucked into plantings.

Previous pages: *Sycamores stand guard at the Norton Simon Museum.* Above: *Watercolor ground plan by Doug Jamieson of the Norton Simon garden.*

We chose Mediterranean plants that mimicked the plants in the Giverny gardens. For weeping willows we used the sacred tree of Mexico, the weeping Montezuma cypress (*Taxodium mucronatum*), a first cousin of my favorite tidewater bald cypress (*Taxodium distichum*). Of course we could grow both tropical and hardy water lilies. Rushes at the edge of the water were local ones. Deciduous tulip poplar (*Liriodendron tulipifera*) from the southeast United States was planted in the café patio, as I knew that the sun would be welcome through the bare winter trees. In the spring, when the days began to heat up, the pale green leaves would come out and cover the terrace.

Mrs. Simon and I talked about special places in the garden for a tryst under a flowering tree. She wanted lots of colorful flowering trees and I wanted their reflections in the pond to be different in each season. Many people are not aware of our Southern California seasons. Although they

Below: The entrance to the Norton Simon Museum, previously hot and glary, was transformed, right, to cool and mysterious. Two Mexican sycamores (Platanus mexicana) *planted in the limestone walk form a gateway to the museum.*

are not as dramatic as those on the East Coast, we definitely have seasons, just more subtle. The changing light is the most obvious difference, from the hot overhead white glare of midsummer, where even red cannot be distinguished, to the beautiful slanted warmth of autumnal light. One of my favorite fall experiences is seeing our native sycamores with their beautiful camouflage bark lit from the side, the rich leather brown of their leaves, some crinkling underfoot, adding to the crisp, dusty dry smell of the season. The golden color of the *Liriodendron* reflected in the pond and the brown and gold grasses tell me it is fall at the Norton Simon.

I persuaded the architects to run the warm ochre French limestone tile flooring outside into the garden and to the entrance stairs in the front. The stone replaced the front walk of hot uncomfortable tarmac and runway lights. I wanted the entrance to be experienced through the dappled light of the new Mexican sycamore (*Platanus mexicana*) grove with a view through the glass grand hall to the pond beyond, which would beckon you into the garden. I placed two trees in the walk as gates, to increase awareness,

encourage you to leave your freeway rage behind, allow you to be open to experiencing the museum and garden. The bronze Rodin sculptures were woven throughout the entrance grove, which made them more mysterious, intimate, and human.

At the San Francisco Flower and Garden Show I found the name of a quarry that had beautiful big pieces of Sierra granite. I flew up to Fresno and drove to the foothills of the Sierra and checked out the quarry, which had recently opened after having been closed since the Depression. It was Sierra granite that was used to replace the damaged buildings of the 1906 San Francisco earthquake and fire. The huge quarried pieces had lain fallow since 1929 and become covered with beautiful mosses. Each one was a work of art. I thought it looked like a Noguchi graveyard! I immediately wanted to use them at the Norton Simon, so I tagged them, and several months later Laurie Lewis, my project designer, and John Sudocan from the museum went up to the quarry with the sizes of all of the sculpture from the collection that would be placed in the garden. They methodically found stones for new

A hard modern pool, left, *was torn out and replaced with a naturally shaped one*, opposite. *Monet's waterlilies in Pasadena are graced by two works by French Catalan sculptor Aristide Maillol:* Mountain *in the center, and* Water *in the distance.*

sculpture bases and benches, stone to be carved out for ashtrays, and huge pieces for the fountain and pond. I felt the more unified the materials in the garden, the more harmonious it would be. The sculpture would be united by bronze and stone and framed by many shapes of green. The green background of the hedges makes the flowering trees stand out just as black velvet sets off a diamond.

There were a few strong and important trees from the original planting. We kept those, and only removed seedlings and disease-weakened trees. We uncovered a stand of silver-trunked eucalyptus (*Eucalyptus citriodora*) that reminded me of the Degas dancers in both the painting and sculpture collections.

I designed the entire garden as a painting, borrowing from the great English painter Turner and the equally famous garden designer Gertrude Jekyll. The center of Turner's paintings was always red—a ship on fire, a sunset or sunrise—and the painting got cooler and cooler as it receded from the center. Jekyll used this technique for her spectacular flowering borders, and I decided I would use it for the entire garden.

An existing flaming coral tree is the center of the garden and from it the flower colors of the plants moved on the right side through oranges, pinks, and yellows to white water lilies, and on the left through infinite shades of blues, lavenders, and grays.

This is a much calmer approach than Monet's riot of color, but it also means you can put lots of different plants with similar-colored flowers together. The overall effect is more harmonious and strong, keeping the garden from looking like crayon-colored confetti. Since then I have used this idea in many of my planting designs.

A great white heron sailed onto the water one day soon after the pond and plants were installed, and his approval let me know that we had built a natural pond just for him.

In fact, the garden has doubled the attendance to the museum and I have witnessed very loud, strung-out children run out into the garden and slowly quiet down as they experience the safe, calm, and natural environment. It works the same way on me, as well as fulfilling one of my lifelong goals.

Previous pages: *Massed daylilies last all summer and their color holds up in the harsh midday light. Across the pond a grove of eucalyptus I call "The Dancers" and Gwynn Murrill's cheetah bronze.* Left: *The museum under construction.* Opposite: *Maillol's* Air *levitating over lavender and backed by heavy dripping curtains of rare Kashmir cypress.* Following pages: *Brilliant orange cannas frame the east view, looking back to the museum.*

Price–Van Breda
Garden

Art maven Dallas
Price called us when James Turrell, the famed sculptor of light, was
building *Sky Space*, an art temple at her house. The oval structure is
vertically clad with the finest clear California redwood and has an
interior of smooth creamy white stucco with an oculus open to the
sky. Price and Turrell designed a comfortable bench of many rare
woods from which to view the changing sky. To the viewer's surprise
and delight, this environment controls the perception of light. Dawn
or dusk emerge as one color and then change to another in a very
slow, hypnotic way. I find it to be a spiritual space, as Price does. She
says she often goes there alone, but the experience can also be shared
with her husband or ten or more friends.

It is located on a steep, precarious slope, as many temples

throughout history have been. The arduous climb, I suspect, was once
the way to heighten your awareness, to make you mindful of where
you were going, and to prepare you for the coming experience.

We looked at the entire hillside and felt that the strong masculine
structure should emerge from a soft planting of waves of grass and fold
into a pattern of plants with strong colors or textures, and that the
new staircase and paths should be made of a complementary stone.
We chose gray-brown sweetwater stone with streaks of rust and black
to replace the railroad tie steps that climbed the hill. The subtle stone
looked handsome with the redwood. To soften the base we planted
Chondropetalum elephantinum, a glaucous South African rush with bracts
the exact color of the redwood around the pavilion.

Crucial to the project was stonemason José Aguirre, whose
family was originally from Zaxatecs, Mexico, and who learned his
craft alongside his father. José and I had been working together almost
twenty years by the time he took on this project. First, to build the
stone fountain located across a deck from Price's dressing room, he
constructed a huge pulley system with the assistance of his brother and
several workers. They then brought all of the stones up the hill one by

Previous pages: *Climbing to
temples in treacherous places is an
age-old tradition. We built new
stone steps to Artist James Turrell's*
Sky Space *oval temple.* Left: *The
hillside before Joe Sturges, a designer
from our studio, worked with José
Aguirre to build the stairs and
fountains.* Opposite: *Ground plan
of the Price–Van Breda Garden.*

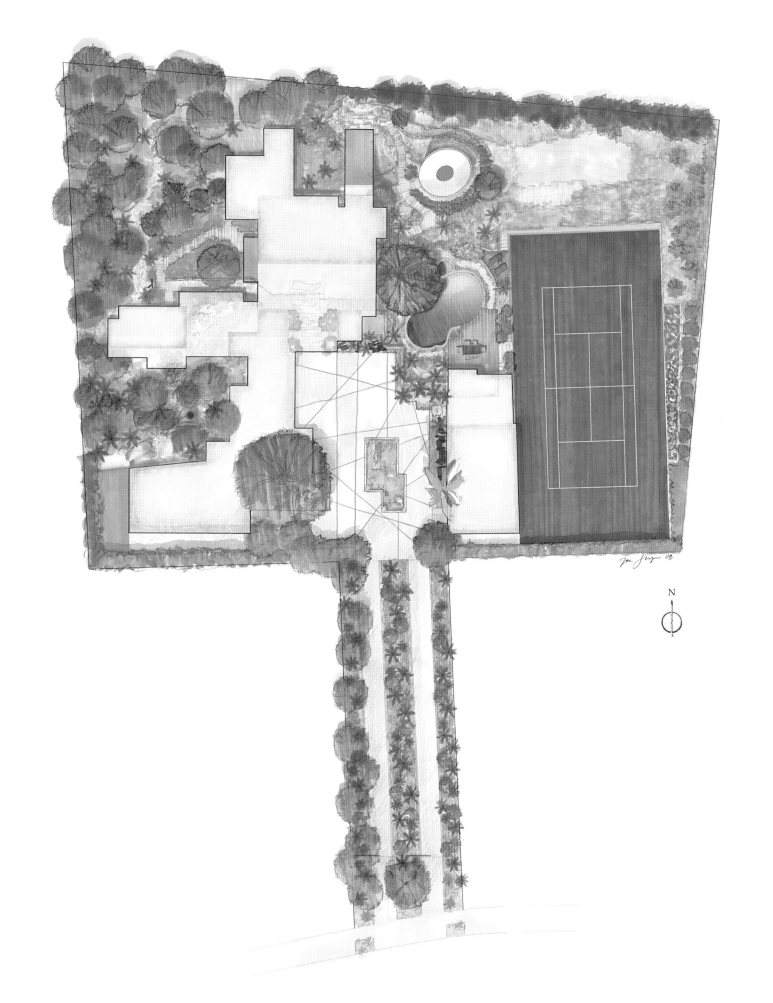

one. Huge boulders had to be wedged into the sides of the hill to contain the soil and to anchor the big slabs for the stone steps. If you started at the bottom, every step could have been chipped or crushed by the huge stones going up the hill. Since they started at the top, the finished stonework was not destroyed by the construction of the stairs.

As the stair neared completion, Price said, "It looks fabulous. Let's do the entrance court and stairs up under the house." At the time these were railroad ties, not nearly as elegant as the house and the art temple. I have never like railroad ties as a building material, partly because I suspect the creosote applied is toxic (although I like its under-the-boardwalk smell reminiscent of my childhood summers). I also feel that as steps railroad ties are too narrow for the foot to be safe, and I find them coarse and inappropriate for most properties.

One day I came to the site to find Howard Formby, one of my project garden designers, playing in the stream with Price! They were in fact designing and placing rocks along and in the stream together. Price is great fun and, having climbed the seven great mountain peaks including the highest, Everest, she is a great sport and will tackle anything she desires with courage, strong opinions, and gusto—qualities that make the process easier for the designer. Chronic indecision takes the life and joy out of a project. Her contemporary art choices reflect this daring as well and are in contrast to the naturalistic style of the garden we planted for the property.

We continued for over a year moving through the entire site, editing overgrown trees and shrubs, adding stone stairs, finding new places to go, and making outdoor spaces. Most of the garden's plants, except for those on the sunny south-facing hill next to the sky piece and tennis court, had to be shade tolerant. In Rustic Canyon's cool climate, we created a riparian garden next to the steps and under the house by using several native ferns and many shades of green groundcovers, moving all of the azaleas next to the stream, and adding tree ferns and native shrubs.

Left and right: *Artist Deborah Butterfield's trompe l'oeil horse, which looks like pieces of wood but is actually cast bronze, stands in a bed of steel-colored fescue. A new steel fence by designer Joe Sturges encloses the swimming pool and makes a background for kangaroo paws and Tasmanian tree ferns.*

Above: *Water from a stream trickles through the garden.*
Left and right: *Replacing the formerly bare hillside, cast-iron plants (a favorite of Victorian grandmothers) and lacy ferns love the dark shade under the bridge.*

Above: *Steps of rough stone slabs with crevices become tiny rock gardens for small maidenhair ferns, violets, and baby tears. Opposite: In the foreground luxuriant jasmine covers the walls of the spa, and its fabulous fragrance scents the air on warm evenings.*

Above: *Strategically placed boulders are sited for perching, for watching all kinds of fauna, and for capturing water. In the background, screens filter the light to the art gallery.* Opposite: *An inviting, secluded swimming pool feels more like a secret watering hole and is great for skinny-dipping.*

Boxenbaum Garden

When local architect Steven Ehrlich phoned to suggest that I collaborate on one of his projects, I leaped at the chance to work with him again. We were friends who had worked well together in the past, so it pleased me tremendously to do so once again.

Steven's assignment was to design a new town house for his clients in a completely different location from their previous home. The Boxenbaum family was exchanging a dark, woodsy home in Rustic Canyon for a modern house on a busy Beverly Hills street corner right across the road from a public school. Steven designs in a very classic way and listens to his clients

and becoming more relaxed as they approached the front door. I envisioned guests and family members as they meandered toward the front door, ascending a vertical height of almost one whole story but unaware of the fact that they were actually climbing stairs to get there. This was accomplished by using very gentle low risers separated by good wide treads to make unobtrusive steps to this gracious off-center entrance.

Even gardens planted in new homes can successfully incorporate the memory of a resident's past gardens without being compromised. This family loved their old canyon house and the memories they had of raising children there. I included a grove of ginkgos, planting only the male species since the female fruit has an unpleasant odor, in the front and back to remind them of their many happy times in Rustic Canyon. Oftentimes in an urban setting like this, it is effective to "borrow" landscape used in the neighborhood. By simply looking across the street, you can get ideas that will, in effect, greatly enhance your landscaping. I

A grove of ginkgos shades the wall of windows

in order to best meet their needs. In this case, some of the Boxenbaums' "requirements" for their new home triggered the need for a subterranean garage, thereby elevating the house. This change in elevation turned into an unplanned opportunity for me to incorporate a variety of levels in the garden, always more interesting than flat space.

My goal for the home was to design an entry garden that would coax visitors gently into shedding their street personality

would advise you to always look out your windows and see what is in your immediate surroundings. From the newly framed-in windows at the Boxenbaums' house, I noticed a cluster of Canary Island pines (*Pinus canariensis*) on the horizon across the street. By introducing these trees on this site, we "trick" the viewer into thinking that the pine trees are all part of the same property. This makes the suburban lot seem larger and, at the same time, helps the house feel grounded in its local context. The more you

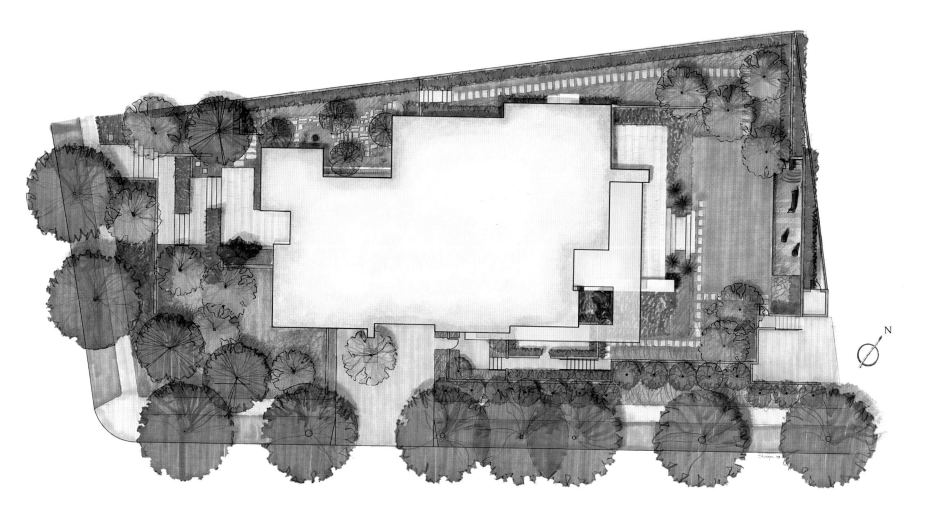

can repeat this, the larger it becomes—repeat for emphasis, as we were taught in grade school.

I also repeated the image of the pine trees' needles by planting rosemary underneath them. Not only did the sharp-edged evergreen foliage of the rosemary mirror the canopy above, but it also kept the plant palette dark and quiet. I tried very hard to use shore creeping juniper with it, but despite careful attention to watering, soil preparation, drainage, and tender loving care,

Previous pages: *Winding gently up almost one story through the garden from the street to the entrance, the broad stone front steps repeat the horizontal planes of the house.* Above: *Ground plan for the Boxenbaum property.*

As designed by Steven Ehrlich, every

Opposite: *A construction photograph shows the side yard before planting; the space has become a tiny garden for Mr. Boxenbaum's office with water burbling in a Chinese rice bowl, a rain chain, and a group of Japanese maples.*
Above: *The covered terrace is perfect for California-style outdoor entertaining.*

window in the house looks into a garden

191

the juniper clearly wasn't meant to be planted in that spot. It was replaced with cotoneaster and a lovely red-tinged sedum, which has been more successful.

Having visited the stone sculpture studio of Isamu Noguchi on Shikoku Island, Japan, I was intrigued by the idea of adding some beautiful stones to the garden. Over tea with Noguchi's stonecutter, now an artist in his own right, I learned a great deal about transforming local stone into abstract sculpture through proper placement and minimal cutting. I found huge pieces of basalt here that were similar to the ones I had seen in Noguchi's studio and garden. Not only did the Boxenbaums encourage me, but they became part of the process, helping me pick out the perfect stones at the Ventura stone yard for the pool in their back garden. The dark basalt stones were placed in the pool against a terra-cotta-colored wall with a concealed water source that helps mask the sounds of the neighboring school and streets. Neighbors like this so much they copied the idea across the street.

The Boxenbaums owned two wooden sculptures that they wanted to include in the garden. While the house was being built, I kept them in my office and really got to know them well; I called them "the greeters." We placed them along the entrance path.

Monumental roughly carved basalt pillars placed in the pond capture light and cast odd shapes on the terra-cotta wall with its background frieze of feathery bamboo.

Art Center
Rooftop Garden

Art Center, a top-ranking art and design college for almost eighty years, is known as a cutting-edge institution that adapts to the changing and challenging needs of modern global culture. Working closely with business, industry, and its local community, it produces some of the most innovative talents in the design field year after year. Art Center had outgrown its hillside campus and needed to expand. It chose a building complex in the light manufacturing district of Pasadena, very close to the new gold line train, the end of the Pasadena freeway, and downtown Los Angeles.

The building complex was built after World War II by Cal Tech for five aircraft companies, including pre-merger McDonnell and Douglas, as the Southern California Cooperative Wind Tunnel. Kevin Daly and Chris Genik, friends of mine from Santa Monica, were the architects hired to reconfigure a rather difficult building for studio space; it had no windows and little light. Their design split open the top of the building and huge sail-like structures became skylights. They asked us to design a roof garden for the building in addition to landscaping the first phase of the new campus.

We had designed one roof garden years ago for the Hermès store in Beverly Hills, and to design a garden for a Daly Genik building was exciting. Kevin had been the lead staff architect in Frank Gehry's office when we both worked on the Schnabel house. During our collaboration we all came up with the idea of the skylight ships sailing through the prairie. A constant breeze flows

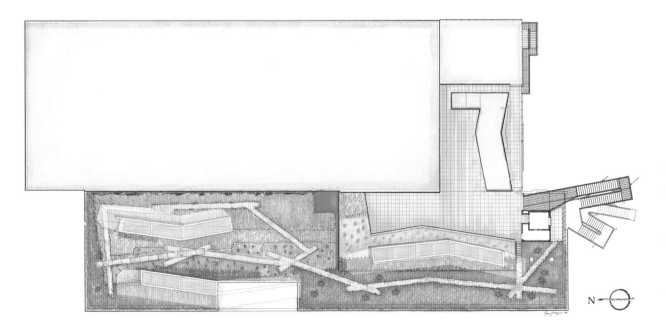

Previous pages: *The skylights that open up the former wind tunnel are huge sail-like structures.* Left: *Plan of the rooftop.* Opposite: *A wall of green vines is a stark contrast to the sleek light structures.*

N

up the arroyo parkway area so the grasses were always moving and changing.

Because of the weight restrictions, we had from as little as 6 inches of soil up to two feet to plant the grasses, miscanthus, and sesleria. Several paths crisscross the garden and there is a bench for watching the sun go down from this dramatic site.

For its use of many innovative sustainable building practices—including our green roof, which helps control the temperature of the building and improves its energy consumption—this Art Center building was awarded LEED (Leadership in Energy and Environmental Design) silver certification.

Below: *The roof of the Art Center before its transformation.*
Right: *Grasses, continually moving and changing, soften the powerful industrial shapes of the building.*

Gardens at Live Oaks

In 1998, I was approached by an East Coast businessman to help create a garden for his new house on the central coast of California. We walked the site together as he talked about his dream house and its gardens. The views to the Pacific and to the local mountains were breathtaking, but the old house had few positive attributes except its location. The older property had been neglected, the landscape around the house had the usual overgrown foundation planting, and the remaining trees, mostly diseased pines, were not significant. The house overlooked a large orchard of cherimoya, avocados, and citrus. Both of us could see the potential. For the owner, the views were the most important; for me, terraces with clear paths to special destinations were the key elements.

The owner and I pored over books on houses and gardens from the golden age of the 1920s, when the financial boom had allowed the wealthy to build seaside summer cottages and winter playgrounds on both the Atlantic and Pacific coasts. Grand tours of Europe had also been very popular, and people spent months in warmer climates along the Mediterranean in France, Italy, and Spain. These tours sparked an interest in the architecture of these beautiful places. Large monographs like *Provincial Houses in Spain* and *Spanish Gardens and Patios* by Mildred Stapley Byne and Arthur Byne were printed in the twenties documenting both the simple and grand architecture of the houses they had seen. These became the pattern books for the new houses the grand tourists would build.

Although the houses on the East Coast were grander than those on the West Coast, both Florida and California had been Spanish territories, so they adapted designs based on their Spanish antecedents. The sprawling white stucco and red tiled roofs of the early adobe ranchos of California were very influential, and simpler rural dwellings were predominant around Santa Barbara.

My client had visited the more palatial houses in Florida and was smitten by architect Addison C. Mizner's Palm Beach houses of the twenties. We talked about potential California architects for his dream house who would understand this vernacular. I suggested three architects, whom he interviewed. His final choice was Buzz Yudell of Moore Ruble Yudell, the internationally acclaimed Santa Monica–based firm, because he thought the firm could make a modern interpretation of the Mizner style. I remember him constantly reminding us that he wanted arches, and that he also wanted the house to be a warm color.

In fact Mizner had built a house in Montecito simpler than any of the Florida houses. The final house Yudell designed had a classic U-shaped plan with central courtyards and clear axial views.

My design for the garden was focused on creating

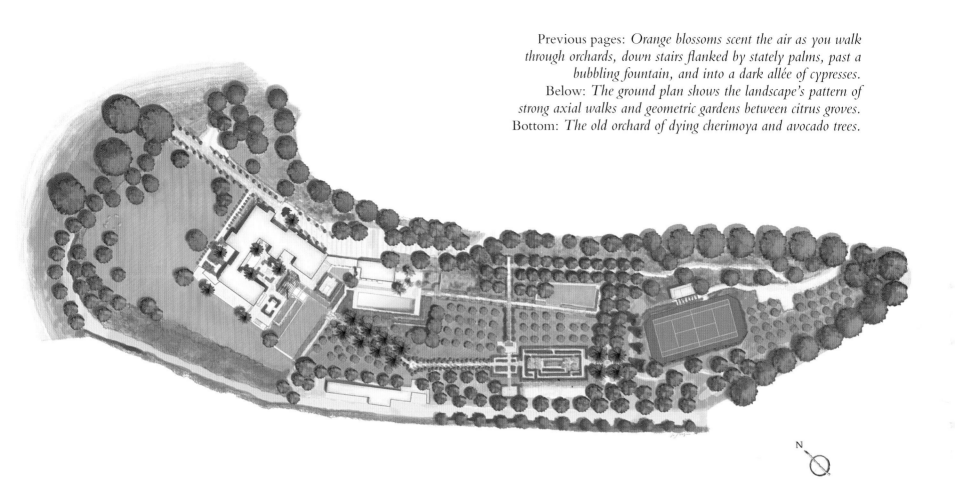

N

different experiences as one walks through it

The emphasis throughout the design was on capturing the views wherever one looked from the house or garden. Yudell and the owner decided to keep the site of the new house on the footprint of the old one as the views to the sea and mountains were the most favorable. Buzz and I worked very carefully to integrate the house and its surroundings.

My design focused on creating different experiences and moments as one walks through the garden. Some of the unifying elements are strong axes running longitudinally north-south and several traversing latitudinally east-west. Use of the similar Santa Barbara stone as the primary building material for walls and terraces and their clear geometry create the seamless effect of their always having been there.

The architect's and owner's choice of keeping the house on a flat part of the site at the top of the slopes gave me the opportunity to terrace the entire property—an ancient way of making the land more usable—and to use many classic building solutions. The terraces create flat plateaus for a dining terrace, a terrace off the living room, a spa terrace, a pool and pool pavilion, a rose garden, a grass terrace overlooking the orchard, a maze, a bocci court, and a palm court. All of the terraces have patterned stone paving using the same Santa Barbara stone with terra-cotta-colored stone or with local river pebbles set in designs to add interest to the steep site. The stairs connecting the terraces are stone as well, and most paths are made of local decomposed granite.

Below: *The original house on its superb hilltop site.*
Right: *The hillside has become a series of gardens and orchards. Stone steps with sizable gravel paths between each flight make both the descent and ascent much easier.*

Once the stone bones of the garden were in place, we added dark green conifer hedges to reinforce the structure, creating rooms and halls. Seasonal flowering trees made bright banners of red and golden yellow throughout the garden. Smaller shrubs and perennials followed the palette of the trees.

Around the perimeter of the property are mass plantings of native shrubs, ceanothus, rhus, arctostaphylos, laurus, with coast live oaks (*Quercus agrifolia*), so the house and its grounds settle seamlessly into their native surroundings. We restored the native plants of the client's adjoining hillside property, removing foreign plants that had seeded there, and tried very carefully not to plant any invasive species in the new gardens.

One enters the property from a local road onto a gravel lane. The entrance to the house parallels the local road, but a stately planting of native coast live oaks shields the view of the house and property from the road as well as establishing the site in its natural context.

I created a series of captivating moments as one enters the property. Through simple columns of Santa Barbara stone and a wrought iron gate, one catches a view across the facade of the main house and out through an allée of Italian cypresses to the nearby

mountains. First one drives into a gravel parking court, and then onto a flagstone main drive flanked by large terra-cotta pots planted with kumquats. Next is a courtyard where a rustic stone trough is surmounted by a fountain mask that vaguely resembles the owner (left). One ventures on axis through another gate, down a green road of cypress lined with agapanthus that frames and captures the view toward the mountains.

The entry to the house and garden was created with a series of courtyards. The first one is for parking under the oaks. Then, as one walks down a wide path paralleling the north facade of the villa with the mountains framed by cypresses, one is drawn to the sound of a tinkling fountain. Once visitors come into the entrance court, they walk up wide generous stairs to the front hall. Here one sees across a central courtyard through handsome steel-framed arched windows to an attached living room pavilion and the first, dramatic view of the Pacific Ocean and the silvery sparkles of light on the water.

The house is organized around a series of courtyards facing southeast to the ocean with views down the coast, and is protected from stiff afternoon winds off the sea by the living room. The central courtyard is the core of the house and has become the main place to relax—to have drinks before a meal or to linger with a

Native coast live oaks mask the house and property

book when the sun is behind the house. The fountain design in this courtyard was influenced by a fountain I particularly like at Scripps College in Claremont, California; its soothing sound and crisp square shape suited this space. I prefer fountains and pools that have gentle steps into them because they are much safer for small children and dogs, and for the most part I have followed this principle throughout the grounds.

An iron dining pergola covered with giant Burmese honeysuckle is sequestered from the cool sea air by placing it four steps below the first courtyard. It looks out over the southwest of the property to the sea. On the left of the dining pergola low clipped hedges hide the spa, which has a framed view straight out to the ocean. Adjoining the spa is another, more intimate, dining terrace covered by a magnificent coral tree; on cool days the fireplace here can be lit to take away the chill of the coastal air.

Next is the pool house. The swimming pool and pavilion are raised just above the grade of the swimming pool terrace, with great views of the garden below and to the far horizon.

The two east-facing long axial paths create vastly different feelings: One leads along the top of the site and has the big horizontal view of the ocean across the orchards, while the other leads to the bottom and goes through a series of allées and varying experiences.

One starts at the top of the hill in a small terrace, with lemon-filled Italian terra-cotta pots on each corner and a bubbling fountain whose stone pebble compass identifies the site's location. Traveling down a stately staircase with an allée of majestic Canary Island palms (*Phoenix canariensis*) surrounded by agaves (*Agave attenuata*), one is sheltered from the sun. To the right of the first allée is the beginning of the citrus orchards, underplanted with California poppies. Next to the orchard is a big stone wall to the right, a perfect place for espaliered figs underplanted with artichokes, both of which are sent back to New York when they are in season, so that the owner can enjoy his California bounty.

I like to vary the quality of light in the garden. The palm-lined staircase, which ends in a clipped Italian cypress roundel that surrounds another stone fountain, makes this landing cooler and the journey down the hill more mysterious as one goes through the dark allée of the cypress. Down a few more stairs one reaches a wide garden parterre rimmed with germander (*Teucrium chamaedrys*) and filled with old roses. The softly colored roses and the brighter light and sudden new views of the larger garden are a surprise. Straight ahead is another dark hedge of clipped redwood (*Sequoia sempervirens*), rarely used as a hedge but once recommended by Elizabeth de Forest. She was the talented wife of the great Santa Barbara landscape architect Lockwood de Forest, who built some of the finest gardens of the twenties, the golden age of garden design in Santa Barbara.

One enters the maze and wanders cautiously on paths between the six-foot hedges with unseen entrances and some dead ends. At the end of the maze one comes out of the dark hedge walls to discover a large lily pond with fish and turtles in the center of a clearing. Two small box-edged parterres flanking it hold yellow flowering cassias underplanted with a dazzling yellow columbine (*Aquilegia chrysantha*),

from the road, placing the site in its natural context

native to Arizona, New Mexico, and adjacent areas in Mexico. I often like to plant different sections of the garden with blossoms in the same color. It makes the picture more harmonious, a special color "happening" with a stronger impact.

Two benches are placed here, allowing one to view the pond life from the shade: A Chinese red dragonfly flits about and then perches on an iris reed, the turtles sun themselves on the exposed warm rocks, the fish swim in and out of their apartment house.

After leaving the maze and the lily pond, one arrives in the secret palm garden, my personal favorite among the garden spaces. Four ancient Canary Island palms with giant feather fronds almost touch over the agave fountain. In my studio, we designed all of the tiles for this fountain, based on favorite things of mine. Central to the fountain is the bronze ceramic agave, which gently dribbles water over its leaves down into the tiled basin. Water trickles over a large periwinkle blue agave into the small tiled trough surrounding the fountain. Some of the details were taken from a William Spratling silver bracelet I own, and the agaves were repeated in carefully colored tiles. This is the most tranquil place in the garden. Sometimes I think we should string up a hammock between the trees—nothing could be nicer than a nap here away from the activity of the big house.

Glancing up the hill, one sees a staircase bordered with olive trees underplanted with white and pink rock roses and lined with springtime periwinkle bluebells. At the terminus of this view is an eighteenth-century oil jar that also ends a wilder path through more olives underplanted with bulbs and snow-in-summer (*Cerastium tomentosum*).

Looking the other way the view stops with a giant agave (*Agave americana*), repeating the theme from the palm garden. Another path on this lower level takes one under a hazy blue tunnel made from Atlas cedar (*Cedrus atlantica 'Glauca Pendula'*) onto the bocci court, which sports a brightly colored flowering perennial border as a surprise after all of the muted greens, grays, and blues of the earlier gardens: fuzzy kangaroo paws (*Anigozanthos*) from Australia, Jerusalem sage (*Phlomis fruiticosa*), and orange African daisy (*Arctotis acaulis*) representing several other zones with similar climates.

A small enclosed courtyard of Monterey cypress (*Cupressus macrocarpa*) clipped as a buttress is the visual terminus for the water staircase that starts at the upper path, splashes down through the orchard, and ends in a tank on a small terrace a couple of steps above the rose garden.

Building the garden for Live Oaks was a great experience for me. I was able to create the design influenced by many of my favorite gardens and adapt elements that delighted me in the older gardens of California and of Europe.

Opposite: *A water staircase crosses the citrus orchard with pots of my favorite* Agave attenuata *on the repeated stone plinths.* Following pages, left: *Details of paving and tile work designed in my studio.* Following pages, right: *In the secret palm court four ancient* Phoenix canariensis *palms, the largest we brought in, surround a fountain centered by a bronze ceramic agave that gently dribbles water into the basin.*

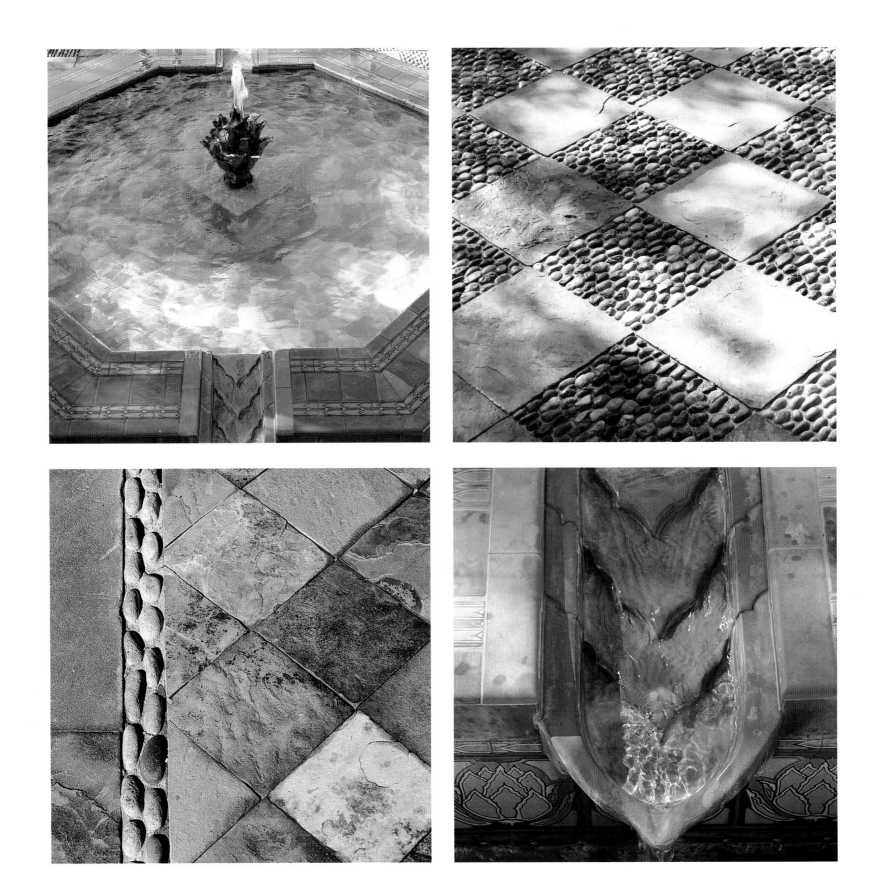

Above: *The lawn where croquet is played has stunning views of the Pacific. While awaiting their turn, players can perch on the surrounding stone bench and sip a glass of Pimm's.* Opposite: *A small courtyard with an off-center lemon tree and low stepped fountain, situated before a large dining pergola covered in Burmese honeysuckle.*

Left: *The pool offers great views of the garden, the sky, and distant Santa Barbara Island.* Opposite: *To cover the cushions on the chaises we found outdoor fabric to match the periwinkle trumpet blossoms of* Thunbergia grandiflora.

Above left: *Reminiscent of the Appian Way, the front drive has a view to the Santa Barbara Mountains.* Above right: *A rustic trail through the ancient olives, which were moved from the Central Valley, is carpeted with snow-in-summer.* Opposite: *An 18th-century French olive jar at the terminus of the stairs from the palm court, with its agave fountain.*

Opposite: *A regal allée of* Phoenix canariensis *palms underplanted with* Agave attenuata *steps down to a pebble-patterned terrace and a softly gurgling fountain before turning into a dark allée of paired Italian cypresses,* above.

Children's Gardens

Opportunities to build children's gardens have come to my firm frequently over the past twenty years, and my interest in them has become a passion-driven mission. Most children today are so electronically wired much of the day that their senses are totally dulled and they are often frantic, failing in school, overweight, and unhealthy. Many have lost the joy and sense of wonder in nature as they are shuttered in the concrete spaces of the city and no longer have the chance to experience the natural world. Richard Louv has written a transforming book, *Last Child in the Woods,* about what he calls Nature Deficit Disorder. He explains that as children we are hardwired to play in mud and water and experience the out of doors. He describes the "diminished use of the senses, attention difficulties, and higher rates of physical and emotional illnesses" that come when that access is denied.

It is essential for children to be exposed to nature, as it creates a sense of well-being and promotes good health. I know that when I am grumpy, slightly down, frenzied, or feel like a trapped animal, I have to get outside. Even walking around the block and smelling the ocean air really helps, but going for a prolonged walk on the beach or in our local Santa Monica Mountains totally restores me. All of my senses go on high alert when I am outside: Food tastes and smells are enhanced, touch is better, and I discover new plants, bugs, colors, and textures. I am also aware of my own safety and of those with me. I am more in tune with my sense of well-being and happiness. I feel myself again.

I really enjoy designing natural places for children to wake up their senses and to enhance their discovery of edible plants that bear fruit, interesting seed pods, strong scents both pleasant and unpleasant (foul smells always get a child's attention). I often use a variety of textures, trees whose leaves change color and fall to the ground, plants that attract caterpillars and butterflies, places to hide and climb, materials like sand and rocks, and always water. Using native plants promotes education, as children are introduced to and learn about their local natural surroundings. I prefer not to have signs or labels of any kind in these natural gardens. We design shady spots for storytelling, lessons, playing music, eating, and dancing. Whenever possible we include places to plant seeds in order to show children where fruits and vegetables come from. Watching busy ants and butterflies, collecting leaves, making a boat out of a seedpod, using pebbles for little houses or cars, playing in the water, and getting dirty: This is our idea of a "hands-on" experience where everything can be touched and explored! In all of our children's gardens we have included a miniature arroyo seco, or dry creek, which replicates the surrounding native landscape.

Most of our gardens are in Southern California, where children can be outside most of the year because of our mild, dry climate. These natural spaces, rather than prefabricated ones, allow children to dream and to use their imaginations to create their own world of memories, images, ideas, and stories.

Previous pages: *A horny toad graces the amphitheater
at Kidspace.* Above: *Students watering their
newly planted pumpkin seeds at the half-acre kitchen
garden of the 24th Street Elementary School, once
an asphalt frying pan next to the I-10 freeway in
downtown Los Angeles.*

Inner-City Arts

Inner-City Arts is located in the heart of downtown Los Angeles's Skid Row, near the produce markets. Most students are children of Mexican and Central American immigrants who live in crowded apartments nearby. They have no access to parks or other outdoor spaces in the neighborhood, which has a large homeless population.

Bob Bates, a now-legendary art teacher, started Inner-City Arts with the help of Irwin Jaeger, Beth Tischler, and the Ahmanson Foundation to fill a gap in arts education. They enlisted architect Michael Maltzan to transform an automotive repair center into a new school for the arts. They invited me to design the landscape around the renovated buildings twenty-five years ago.

Bates had the children draw their fantasy of the courtyard garden to be, and most of the children drew palm trees, orange trees, brightly colored flowers, and volcanoes. Initially stumped by the volcanoes, we finally came up with a fountain that spouted water to represent a volcano. The fountain became the activity center of the courtyard and is used by the students to get water, wash their brushes, and have fun. We added huge date palms (*Phoenix canariensis*) and a few very tall native California fan palms for shade.

I broke into tears a year later when I saw the humble gray poured-in-place fountain decorated with festive, brightly glazed tiles, and carved clay animal head spouts that the children had made.

When we worked again on the 2008 expansion of the school with Maltzan, we wanted the children to have direct contact with trees and edible plants, so we planted apricot, plum, peach, and apple trees. We placed a bed of strawberries that we call "Strawberry Fields" and a cherry tomato patch next to small stone seats.

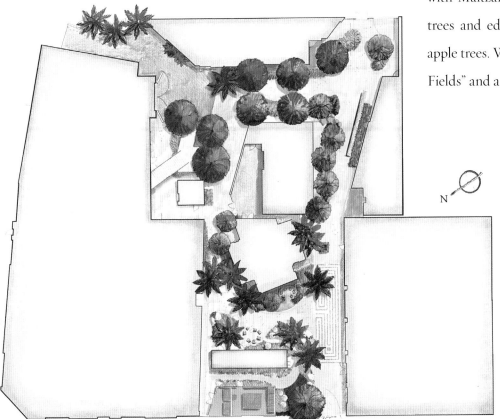

N

Left: *Ground plan of Inner-City Arts.* Opposite, clockwise from top left: *Inner-City Arts is a shining beacon on Skid Row. Children play next to a tiled panel they made in the ceramics building. The palm-shaded courtyard where they have outdoor sketching classes. Picking cherry tomatoes in the courtyard garden.*

Kidspace

Michael Maltzan restored and renovated three dilapidated buildings of a former horticultural center to become the new home of the Kidspace Children's Museum in Pasadena. Since we had successfully worked together on Inner-City Arts, he asked me to join him again on Kidspace.

Behind the museum were several uncultivated acres, which we turned into a garden that still retains its wild feeling. This introduces children to their local natural environment and allows them to explore small trails, discover bumpy or fuzzy plantings, and smell the intoxicating fragrance of blue sage (*Salvia clevelandii*) as they scamper up stone steps into the butterfly garden, where California milkweed (*Asclepias californica*) attracts monarch butterflies to lay their eggs. Butterfly bushes (*Buddleja davidii*), a magnet for all butterflies, hang their purple spires over a path.

We turned a natural bowl into an amphitheater and planted our native sycamore (*Platanus racemosa*) for summer shade when the canyon becomes hot and dry. In the winter it drops its leaves, allowing the sun to warm the chilly spot.

I love to build with natural materials. An arched tunnel made of native bent willows snakes around the hill. Purposely scaled at 5 feet 6 inches, the tunnel forces many adults to stoop, while children run through spontaneously. A small clearing with a sandy bottom has a spiderweb rope for climbing and playing in the sand below.

In Los Angeles much of our wilderness has been paved over and pushed farther back by sprawling suburbs, and our inner city has very few safe parks: Our children have little opportunity to play outside in a wild area. Here is a safe place where children can run freely in a natural habitat and where parents feel comfortable letting them play.

Above: *Ground plan of Kidspace.* Opposite: *The living willow walk and the rope spiderweb are our favorite places at Kidspace. Tricycles race around the track near a pergola covered with purple wisteria in the spring.*

Garden School Foundation

Five years ago I was asked to help with a garden plan for the 24th Street Elementary School in South L.A. near the University of Southern California. This once-distinguished neighborhood had been torn apart in the sixties by the extension of the I-10 freeway, and the school's green playing fields and gardens had been covered with asphalt.

Noticing that the playground was very hot, often polluted, and had no trees or greenery, several neighborhood women became concerned about the children. These neighbors formed a group with sympathetic teachers at the school and friends including local chefs, journalists, a kitchen and garden designer. They were determined to change the conditions at the school, and when the opportunity arose they acted immediately.

Learning that the entire schoolyard was going to be replaced with more asphalt by the Los Angeles Unified School District, the group asked me to design a professional plan to submit to the LAUSD board. With a half-acre kitchen garden, a new track surrounding a grass playing field, and the one-third-acre California Native Garden, our plan convinced LAUSD to remove the asphalt for these projects. Although they planted a row of large Canary Island pines (*Pinus canariensis*) and a mixed hedgerow along the freeway (part of our plan as well), there was no money to plant the gardens.

The nonprofit Garden School Foundation was formed to raise money and was helped by Nancy Silverton, founder of La Brea Bakery; John Yamin, CEO of La Brea Bakery; and many other chefs in town. We visited Alice Waters' Edible Schoolyard in Berkeley, whose Chez Panisse Foundation advised us on how to start. Carolyn Doepke Bennett and the Hancock Park Garden Club helped us obtain a $25,000 award.

We have since become serious advocates for kitchen gardens to teach young children the pleasures and nutritional benefits of growing and eating their own food. One thousand children have classes in these two outdoor classrooms. Each class has its own plot, and in the native garden third- and fourth-grade students study California history, geology, biology, and the ethno-botanical history of the Native Americans.

As Richard Louv says, "we must ensure that children in every kind of neighborhood have everyday access to natural spaces, places, and experiences."

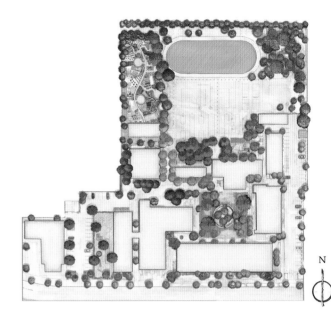

N

Top: *Ground plan for the welcoming schoolyard that has replaced a dreary asphalt playground, above.* Opposite: *Children paint the garden shed and work in the garden.*

Favorite Trees and Plants

FAVORITE TREES

Acacia baileyana 'Purpurea'
Acacia melanoxylon
Agathis robusta
Arbutus 'Marina'
Arbutus unedo
Archontophoenix cunninghamiana
Brachychiton acerifolium
Brachychiton discolor
Brahea armata
Brahea edulis
Brugmansia 'Betty Marshall'
Brugmansia 'Charles Grimaldi'
Butia capitata
Calodendrum capense
Cassia leptophylla
Cedrus atlantica 'Glauca Pendula'
Cedrus deodara
Cercis canadensis 'Forest Pansy'
Cupressus cashmeriana
Cupressus macrocarpa
Cupressus sempervirens
Cussonia paniculata var. sinuata
Dracaena draco
Erythrina caffra
Erythrina coralloides 'Bicolor'
Erythrina crista-galli
Erythrina x bidwillii
Erythrina x sykesii
Eucalyptus citriodora
Eucalyptus deglupta
Eucalyptus ficifolia
Eucalyptus nicholii
Eucalyptus sideroxylon
Grevillea robusta
Jacaranda mimosifolia
Jubaea chilensis
Koelreuteria bipinnata
Laurus nobilis
Leptospermum laevigatum

Leucadendron argenteum
Liriodendron tulipifera
Livistona chinensis
Lophostemon confertus
Magnolia grandiflora
Magnolia grandiflora 'Blanchard'
Magnolia grandiflora 'Little Gem'
Markhamia hildebrandtii
Melaleuca linariifolia
Melaleuca nesophila
Metrosideros excelsa
Olea europea
Phoenix canariensis
Phoenix dactylifera
Phoenix reclinata
Phoenix roebelenii
Pinus canariensis
Pinus pinea
Pinus torreyana
Platanus mexicana
Platanus racemosa
Quercus agrifolia
Quercus engelmannii
Quercus lobata
Quercus tomentella
Robinia pseudoacacia 'Frisia'
Schinus molle
Senna splendida 'Ray's Splendor'
Spathodea campanulata
Stenocarpus sinuatus
Tabebuia chrysotricha
Tabebuia impetiginosa
Taxodium mucronatum
Tecoma stans
Thevetia thevetioides
Tipuana tipu
Toona sinensis
Umbellularia californica
Washingtonia filifera
Washingtonia robusta

FAVORITE SHRUBS, PERENNIALS, GRASSES, AND GROUNDCOVERS

Acanthus mollis
Agapanthus 'Storm Cloud'
Anemone japonica (Anemone x hybrida 'Honorine Jobert')
Anigozanthos flavidus
Anigozanthos 'Red Cross'
Arctostaphylos densiflora 'Howard McMinn'
Arctostaphylos manzanita 'Dr. Hurd'
Baccharis pilularis 'Twin Peaks'
Bambusa oldhamii
Banksia praemorsa
Brugmansia 'Betty Marshall'
Brugmansia 'Charles Grimaldi'
Camellia japonica 'Mrs. D.W. Davis'
Camellia sasanqua 'White Dove'
Carex glauca
Carex tumulicola
Carpenteria californica
Ceanothus 'Concha'
Ceanothus griseus horizontalis 'Yankee Point'
Ceanothus 'Ray Hartman'
Cerastium tomentosum
Cistus x purpureus
Clivia miniata
Convolvulus sabatius
Cordyline baueri
Coreopsis grandiflora 'Domino'
Cotoneaster dammeri 'Coral Beauty'
Dianella tasmanica
Digitalis purpurea
Echium fastuosum
Eleagnus pungens 'Fruitlandii'
Eriogonum giganteum
Euphorbia characias 'Bruce's Dwarf'
Euphorbia characias wulfenii

Fragaria chiloensis
Fremontodendron californicum
Gardenia augusta
Gazania 'Aztec Queen'
Garrya elliptica
Geranium 'Johnson's Blue'
Geranium 'Roxanne'
Geranium x cantabrigiense 'Biokovo'
Globularia x indubia
Hedychium gardnerianum
Helichrysum petiolare 'Limelight'
Helleborus argutifolius
Helleborus orientalis
Heteromeles arbutifolia
Heuchera maxima
Hydrangea macrophylla 'Nikko Blue'
Hydrangea quercifolia
Iris 'Babbling Brook'
Iris douglasiana
Iris 'Grandma's Purple Flag'
Iris 'Victoria Falls'
Isoplexis canariensis
Juncus patens
Lavandula dentata candicans
Lavandula stoechas 'Otto Quast'
Lavandula x intermedia 'Provence'
Leonotis leonurus
Leucadendron 'Safari Sunset'
Leucojum aestivum
Miscanthus transmorrisonensis
Muhlenbergia capillaris
Muhlenbergia rigens
Olea europaea 'Little Ollie'
Pelargonium sidoides
Pelargonium tomentosum
Philadelphus mexicanus
Phlomis fruticosa
Phormium tenax
Phormium tenax 'Atropurpureum'
Phyllostachys nigra

Pittosporum tobira 'Wheeler's Dwarf'
Polystichum polyblepharum
Rhamnus californica 'Eve Case'
Rhaphiolepis indica 'Clara'
Romneya coulteri
Rosa 'Brandy'
Rosa 'Mutabilis'
Rosmarinus officinalis 'Irene'
Rosmarinus officinalis 'Tuscan Blue'
Salvia 'Allen Chickering'
Soleirolia soleirolii
Strelitzia nicolai
Strelitzia reginae
Teucrium fruticans
Teucrium x lucidrys
Thymus serpyllum 'Elfin'
Westringia fruticosa
Zephyranthes candida

FAVORITE SUCCULENTS
Aeonium arboreum 'Zwartkop'
Aeonium 'Mint Saucer'
Agave americana
Agave attenuata
Agave attenuata 'Nova'
Agave shawii
Aloe arborescens
Aloe marlothii
Dudleya brittonii
Kalanchoe beharensis
Sedum brevifolium
Sedum nussbaumerianum
Senecio mandraliscae

FAVORITE VINES
Aloe ciliaris
Beaumontia grandiflora
Bougainvillea 'California Gold'
Clematis armandii
Clematis 'Avalanche'

Dalechampia dioscoreifolia
Distictis buccinatoria
Distictis laxiflora
Distictis 'Rivers'
Hedera helix 'Hahn's'
Ipomoea indica [I. acuminata]
Jasminum angulare
Jasminum grandiflorum
Jasminum polyanthum
Jasminum tortuosum
Lonicera hildebrandiana
Lonicera japonica 'Halliana'
Pandorea jasminoides 'Alba'
Parthenocissus henryana
Passiflora 'Coral Seas'
Petrea volubilis
Pyrostegia venusta
Rosa banksiae 'Alba Plena'
Rosa 'Belle Portugaise'
Rosa 'Cl. Cecile Brünner'
Rosa 'Mermaid'
Rosa 'Mme Alfred Carriere'
Rosa 'Sombreuil'
Solanum wendlandii
Thunbergia grandiflora
Thunbergia gregorii
Trachelospermum asiaticum
Trachelospermum jasminoides
Vitis californica 'Roger's Red'
Wisteria sinensis 'Cook's Purple'

FAVORITE AQUATIC PLANTS
Marsilea quadrifolia
Nymphaea 'Sir Galahad'
Nymphaea 'Tina'
Pontederia lancifolia
Typha angustifolia

Suggested Reading

Anderson, M. Kat. *Tending the Wild: Native American Knowledge and the Management of California's Natural Resources.* Berkeley: University of California Press, 2005.

Andree, Herb, and Noel Young. *Santa Barbara Architecture.* Santa Barbara, CA: Capra Press, 1980.

Angier, Belle Sumner. *The Garden Book of California.* San Francisco: Paul Elder and Co., 1906.

Belloli, Jay, ed. *Myron Hunt, 1868–1952: The Search for a Regional Architecture.* California Architecture and Architects Series, no. 4. Los Angeles: Hennessey & Ingalls, 1984.

Belloli, Jay, ed., et al. *Johnson, Kaufmann, and Coate: Partners in the California Style.* Santa Barbara, CA: Capra Press, 1992.

Berry, Wendell. *The Art of the Commonplace: The Agrarian Essays of Wendell Berry.* Edited by Norman Wirzba. Washington, DC: Shoemaker & Hoard, 2002.

Birnbaum, Charles A., and Stephanie S. Foell, eds. *Shaping the American Landscape: New Profiles from the Pioneers of American Landscape Design Project.* Charlottesville: University of Virginia Press, 2009.

Bissell, Ervanna Bowen. *Glimpses of Santa Barbara and Montecito Gardens.* Santa Barbara, CA: Schauer Printing, 1926.

Bornstein, Carol, David Fross, and Bart O'Brien. *California Native Plants for the Garden.* Los Olivos, CA: Cachuma Press, 2005.

Brenzel, Kathleen Norris, ed. *Sunset Western Garden Book.* Menlo Park, CA: Sunset Pub. Corp., 8th ed. 2007.

Burle Marx, Roberto. *The Lyrical Landscape.* Berkeley: University of California Press, 2001.

Byne, Arthur, and Mildred Stapley Byne. *Spanish Gardens and Patios.* Philadelphia: J. B. Lippincott Co., 1928.

Cave, Yvonne. *Succulents for the Contemporary Garden.* Portland, OR: Timber Press, 2003.

Chandler, Philip E. *Reference Lists of Ornamental Plants for Southern California Gardens.* Los Angeles: Southern California Horticultural Society, 1993.

Church, Thomas D., et al. *Gardens Are for People.* New York: McGraw-Hill, 1983.

Cornell, Ralph D. *Conspicuous California Plants.* Pasadena, CA: San Pasqual Press, 1938.

Cornett, James W. *How Indians Used Desert Plants.* Palm Springs, CA: Nature Trails Press, 2002.

Dickey, Page. *Gardens in the Spirit of Place.* New York: Stewart, Tabori & Chang, 2005.

Dobyns, Winifred Starr. *California Gardens.* New York: MacMillan, 1931.

Eckbo, Garrett. *Landscape for Living.* New York: Architectural Record with Duell, Sloan and Pearce, 1950.

Flint, Mary Louise, and Steve H. Dreistadt. *Natural Enemies Handbook: The Illustrated Guide to Biological Pest Control.* Oakland, CA: UC Division of Agriculture and Natural Sciences; Berkeley: University of California Press, 1998.

Gardner, Howard. *Frames of Mind: The Theory of Multiple Intelligences.* New York: Basic Books, 1983, reprinted 1993.

———. *The Unschooled Mind: How Children Think and How Schools Should Teach.* New York: Basic Books, 1991.

Garnett, Porter. *Stately Homes of California.* Boston: Little, Brown, 1915.

Gebhard, David, and Robert Winter. *A Guide to Architecture in Los Angeles and Southern California.* Layton, UT: Peregrine Smith, 1977.

Gildemeister, Heidi. *Gardening the Mediterranean Way.* New York, Harry N. Abrams, 2004.

Goldsmith, Margaret Olthof. *Designs for Outdoor Living.* New York: George W. Stewart, 1941.

Goodhue, Bertram Grosvenor. *The Architecture and the Gardens of the San Diego Exposition.* San Francisco: Paul Elder and Co., 1916.

Griswold, Mac, and Eleanor Welles. *The Golden Age of American Gardens: Proud Owners, Private Estates, 1890–1940.* New York: Harry N. Abrams, 1991.

Hanson, A. E. *An Arcadian Landscape: The California Gardens of A. E. Hanson, 1920–1932.* Edited by David Gebhard and Sheila Lynds. Los Angeles: Hennessey & Ingalls, 1985.

Harrison, Robert Pogue. *Gardens: An Essay on the Human Condition.* Chicago: University of Chicago Press, 2008.

Hertrich, William. *The Huntington Botanical Gardens, 1905–1949.* San Marino, CA: Huntington Library, 1949.

Jackson, Wes. *Becoming Native to This Place.* Lexington, KY: University Press of Kentucky, 1994.

Jacson, Helen Hunt. *Ramona.* Boston: Roberts Brothers, 1884.

Johnson, Wendy. *Gardening at the Dragon's Gate.* New York: Bantam Books, 2008.

Keator, Glenn. *Native Perennials of California.* San Francisco: Chronicle Books, 1990.

Longstreth, Richard. *On the Edge of the World: Four Architects in San Francisco at the Turn of the Century.* Cambridge, MA: MIT Press, 1983.

Louv, Richard. *Last Child in the Woods: Saving Our Children From Nature-Deficit Disorder.* Updated and expanded edition. Chapel Hill, NC: Algonquin Books of Chapel Hill, 2008.

Mathias, Mildred E., ed. *Color for the Landscape: Flowering Plants for Subtropical Climates.* Arcadia, CA: California Arboretum Foundation, 1964.

————. *Flowering Plants in the Landscape.* Berkeley: University of California Press, 1982.

McLaren, John. *Gardening in California.* San Francisco: A. M. Robertson, 1908; 2d ed. 1927.

————. *Gardening in California: Landscape and Flower.* San Francisco: A. M. Robertson, 1909.

McWilliams, Carey. *Southern California Country: An Island on the Land.* Layton, UT: Peregrine Smith, 1946; reprint 1983.

Mitchell, Stanley B. *Gardening in California.* New York: Doubleday Doran, 1936.

Moore, Charles, et al. *The Poetics of Gardens.* Cambridge, MA: MIT Press, 1988.

Muller, Katherine K., et al. *Trees of Santa Barbara.* Santa Barbara, CA: Santa Barbara Botanic Garden, 1974.

Munz, Philip A. *A Flora of Southern California.* Berkeley: University of California Press, 1974.

Murmann, Eugene O. *California Gardens.* Los Angeles: Eugene O. Murmann, 1914.

Myrick, David F. *Montecito and Santa Barbara.* Vol. I: *From Farms to Estates.* Vol. II: *The Days of the Great Estates.* Glendale, CA: Trans-Anglo Books, 1988, 1991.

Newcomb, Rexford. *The Spanish House for America.* Philadelphia: J. B. Lippincott Co., 1927.

————. *The Old Mission Churches and Historic Houses of California.* Philadelphia: J. B. Lippincott Co., 1925.

O'Brien, Bart, Betsey Landis, and Ellen Mackey. *Care & Maintenance of Southern California Native Plant Gardens.* Los Angeles: Metropolitan Water District of Southern California, 2006.

Padilla, Victoria. *Southern California Gardens: An Illustrated History.* Berkeley: University of California Press, 1961.

Pavlik, Bruce M., Pamela C. Muick, Sharon G. Johnson, and Marjorie Popper. *Oaks of California.* Los Olivos, CA: Cachuma Press, 1993.

Platt, Charles Adams. *Italian Gardens.* New York: Harper and Brothers, 1894.

Pollan, Michael. *In Defense of Food.* New York: Penguin Press, 2008.

————. *The Omnivore's Dilemma: A Natural History of Four Meals.* New York: Penguin Press, 2006.

————. *Second Nature: A Gardener's Education.* New York: Atlantic Monthly Press, 1991.

Polyzoides, Stefanos, Roger Sherwood, James Tice, and Julius Shulman. *Courtyard Housing in Los Angeles.* Berkeley: University of California Press, 1982.

Power, Nancy Goslee. *The Gardens of California: Four Centuries of Design from Mission to Modern.* New York: Clarkson Potter, 1995. Reprinted with permission, Santa Monica, CA: Hennessey + Ingalls, 2002, 2004.

Roberts, Fred M. *Illustrated Guide to the Oaks of the Southern Californian Floristic Province: The Oaks of Coastal Southern California and Northwestern Baja California, Mexico.* Encinitas, CA: F.M. Roberts Publications, 1995.

Shepherd, John Chiene, and Geoffrey Alan Jellicoe. *Italian Gardens of the Renaissance.* New York: Scribner's, 1925; reprint, London: Tiranti, 1966.

Smithen, Jan. *Sun-Drenched Gardens: The Mediterranean Style.* New York: Harry N. Abrams, 2002.

Starr, Kevin. *Americans and the California Dream, 1850–1915.* New York: Oxford University Press, 1973.

————. *Coast of Dreams: California on the Edge, 1990–2003.* New York: Knopf, 2004.

Staub, Jack. *75 Remarkable Fruits for Your Garden.* Layton, UT: Gibbs Smith, 2007.

Streatfield, David C. *California Gardens: Creating a New Eden.* New York: Abbeville Press, 1994.

————. "The Evolution of the California Landscape." *Landscape Architecture* 130. Parts 1–4: "Settling into Arcadia" (January 1976), pp. 39–46; "Arcadia Compromised" (March 1976), pp. 117–26; "The Great Promotions" (May 1977), pp. 229–49; "Suburbia at the Zenith" (September 1977), pp. 417–24.

Tilford, Gregory L. *Edible and Medicinal Plants of the West.* Missoula, MT: Mountain Press Pub., 1997.

Walliser, Jessica. *Good Bug, Bad Bug: Who's Who, What They Do, and How to Manage Them Organically (All You Need to Know About the Insects in Your Garden).* Pittsburgh, PA: St. Lynn's Press, 2008.

Waters, George, and Nora Harlow. *The Pacific Horticulture Book of Western Gardening.* Boston: David R. Godine, 1991.

Weiskamp, Herbert. *Beautiful Homes and Gardens in California.* New York: Harry N. Abrams, 1964.

Wharton, Edith. *Italian Villas and their Gardens.* New York: Century, 1905.

Williams, Bunny. *On Garden Style.* New York: Simon & Schuster Editions, 1998.

Yoch, James J. *Landscaping the American Dream: The Gardens and Film Sets of Florence Yoch, 1890–1972.* New York: Harry N. Abrams, 1989.

Resources

RETAIL SHOPS

DAO (Design Around Objects)
8767 Beverly Boulevard
Los Angeles, CA 90048
Tel: 310-289-8717
Fax: 310-289-8718
www.daohome.com

The Gardener
1836 Fourth Street
Berkeley, CA 94710
Tel: 510-548-4545
Fax: 510-548-6357
www.thegardener.com

Gurley Antiques
512 South Fair Oaks Avenue
Pasadena, CA 91105
Tel: 626-432-4811
www.gurleyantiques.com

Hervé Baume
19 ter, Rue Petite Fusterie
84000 Avignon
France
www.herve-baume.com

Hollyhock
817 Hilldale Avenue
West Hollywood, CA 90069
Tel: 310-777-0100
Fax: 310-777-0110
www.hollyhockinc.com

Inner Gardens
6050 West Jefferson Boulevard
Los Angeles, CA 90016
Tel: 310-838-8378
Fax: 310-838-7694
www.innergardens.com

Kenneth Lynch & Sons
114 Willenbrock Road
Oxford, CT 06478
Tel: 203-264-2831
Fax: 203-264-2833
www.klynchandsons.com

Nathan Turner Antiques
636 North Almont Drive
West Hollywood, CA 90069
Tel: 310-275-1209

Reborn Antiques
853 North La Cienega Boulevard
Los Angeles, CA 90069
Tel: 310-289-7785
Fax: 310-360-1383
www.rebornantiques.net

Sollano 16
Calle Sollano 16
San Miguel de Allende
Guanajuato, Mexico
Tel: 888-858-3824

Treillage Ltd.
418 East 75th Street
New York, NY 10021
Tel: 212-535-2288
Fax: 212-517-6589
www.treillageonline.com

William Laman
1496 East Valley Road
Montecito, CA 93108
Tel: 805-969-2840
Fax: 805-969-2839
www.williamlaman.com

NURSERIES

To the Trade

Berylwood Tree Farm
1048 East La Loma Avenue
Somis, CA 93066
Tel: 805-485-7601

FK Nursery
2027 Colby Avenue
Los Angeles, CA 90025
Tel: 310-478-0538
Fax: 310-477-2602

Greenlee Nursery
6075 #C Kimball Avenue
Chino, CA 91708
Tel: 909-342-6201
Fax: 909-342-6121
www.greenleenursery.com

Monrovia
18331 East Foothill Boulevard
Azusa, CA 91702
Tel: 800-999-9321
www.monrovia.com

Native Sons
379 West El Campo Road
Arroyo Grande, CA 93420
Tel: 805-481-5996
Fax: 805-489-1991
www.nativeson.com

Orange County Nursery
5485 Grimes Canyon Road
Moorpark, CA 93021
Tel: 800-569-0169
Fax: 805-517-1213
www.ocnursery.com

San Marcos Growers
125 South San Marcos Road
Santa Barbara, CA 93111
Tel: 805-683-1561
Fax: 805-964-1329
www.smgrowers.com

Open to the Public

Merrihew's Sunset Gardens
1526 Ocean Park Boulevard
Santa Monica, CA 90405
Tel: 310-452-1051
Fax: 310-452-2392

Sunset Nursery
4368 West Sunset Boulevard
Los Angeles, CA 90029
Tel: 323-661-1642
Fax: 323-661-9388

Theodore Payne Foundation
10459 Tuxford Street
Sun Valley, CA 91352
Tel: 818-768-1802
Fax: 818-768-5215
www.theodorepayne.org

Tree of Life
33201 Ortega Highway
P.O. Box 635
San Juan Capistrano, CA 92675
Tel: 949-728-0685
Fax: 949-728-0509
www.californianativeplants.com

TILE AND CERAMICS

To the Trade

Ann Sacks
8935 Beverly Boulevard
Los Angeles, CA 90048
Tel: 310-273-0700
Fax: 310-273-0800
www.annsacks.com

Asian Ceramics Inc.
2800 Huntington Drive
Duarte, CA 91010
Tel: 626-449-6800
Fax: 626-449-6895
www.asian-ceramics.com

Campo de' Fiori
1815 North Main Street, Route 7
Sheffield, MA 01257
Tel: 413-528-1857
www.campodefiori.com

Cavendish Grey
8443 Melrose Avenue
Los Angeles, CA 90069
Tel: 323-653-2230
Fax: 323-653-2319
www.cavendishgrey.com

Collezione
Tel: 650-327-1342
Fax: 650-462-0706
www.collezioneusa.com

Country Floors
8735 Melrose Avenue
Los Angeles, CA 90069
Tel: 800-311-9995
Fax: 310-659-6470
www.countryfloors.com

Exquisite Surfaces Tile and Stone
731 North La Cienega Boulevard
Los Angeles, CA 90069
Tel: 310-659-4580
Fax: 310-659-4585
www.xsurfaces.com

Goodwin International
3121 South Oak Street
Santa Ana, CA 92707
Tel: 800-600-3200
Fax: 714-241-1874
www.goodwininternational.com

Malibu Ceramic Works
P.O. Box 1406
Topanga, CA 90290
Tel: 310-455-2485
Fax: 310-455-4385
www.malibuceramicworks.com

Seibert & Rice
P.O. Box 365
Short Hills, NJ 07078
Tel: 973-467-8266
Fax: 973-379-2536
www.seibert-rice.com

OUTDOOR FABRICS AND FURNITURE

To the Trade

Cowtan & Tout
8687 Melrose Avenue, Suite B647
West Hollywood, CA 90069
Tel: 310-659-1423
Fax: 310-659-7332
www.cowtan.com

David Sutherland Showroom
8687 Melrose Avenue, Suite B182
West Hollywood, CA 90069
Tel: 310-360-1777
Fax: 310-289-7756
www.davidsutherlandshowroom.com

Donghia, Inc.
8687 Melrose Avenue, Suite G196
West Hollywood, CA 90069
Tel: 310-657-6060
Fax: 310-657-8453
www.donghia.com

Holly Hunt
8686 Melrose Avenue, Suite B377
West Hollywood, CA 90069
Tel: 310-659-3776
Fax: 310-659-7253
www.hollyhunt.com

Janus et Cie
8687 Melrose Avenue, Suite B193
West Hollywood, CA 90069
Tel: 310-652-7090
Fax: 310-652-1284
www.janusetcie.com

Landscapeforms
Tel: 800-521-2546
Fax: 269-381-3455
www.landscapeforms.com

McKinnon and Harris, Inc.
1806 Summit Avenue
Richmond, VA 23230
Tel: 804-358-2385
Fax: 804-355-7082
www.mckinnonharris.com

Munder-Skiles
872 Madison Avenue #2B
New York, NY 10021
Tel: 212-717-0150
Fax: 212-717-0149
www.munder-skiles.com

Summit Furniture, Inc.
8687 Melrose Avenue, Suite B135
West Hollywood, CA 90069
Tel: 310-289-1266
Fax: 310-289-1257
www.summitfurniture.com

STONE

Bourget Flagstone Co.
1636 11th Street
Santa Monica, CA 90404
Tel: 310-829-4010, ext. 721
www.bourgetbros.com

Malibu Stone & Masonry Supply
3730 Cross Creek Road
Malibu, CA 90265
Tel: 310-456-9444
www.malibustonemasonry.com

LIGHTING

To the Trade

Louis Poulsen
3260 Meridian Parkway
Fort Lauderdale, FL 33331
Tel: 954-349-2525
Fax: 954-349-2550
www.louispoulsen.com

Open to the Public

FX Luminaire
www.fxl.com

Acknowledgments

I am involved with a family of friends: artists, designers, artisans, teachers, cooks, musicians, writers, editors, talented advisors, accountants, housekeepers, gardeners, a master yoga teacher, girlfriends, boyfriends, various four-legged pals, a doctor or two, and visionary friends, without whom my life's work would not be accomplished. I value all of them equally for their trusted work, advice, and respect for what we do together as a team and also for the ability to have fun while working toward a common goal, even when I demand excellence for all that we try to do.

Building and caring for gardens takes a community of friends working together to keep our treasured art form alive. All of us are committed to living a sustainable existence in every way we can. I thank everyone who participates with me in these many endeavors.

Making this book has been a long process and I want to thank my current studio staff first for all of the extra help that they have extended to *Power of Gardens* on top of their daily work. From the bottom of my heart I thank Linda Jassim and Marcia Lee, who have worked tirelessly on the project in every capacity imaginable. Many thanks to Joe Sturges, who has redone all of the plans of the gardens in the book and made them works of art.

My book designer, Doug Turshen, who put up with all of our constant changes and delays, for his keen eye, artistry, and patience with us, and to David Huang, his associate.

The four talented photographers of the book: Marcia Lee, Victoria Pearson, Lisa Romerin, and Tim Street-Porter, who were so willing to capture my vision.

Everyone at Stewart, Tabori & Chang, who were so gracious to work with, especially Leslie Stoker, Jennifer Levesque, and Kate Norment.

Last to my son, Oliver, a brilliant film editor, who constantly encouraged and challenged me to go to a higher level of excellence.

Index

Note: Page numbers in *italics* refer to illustrations.

Photography Credits

NGPA Staff: 16–17, 20, 22 (b&w), 26 (b&w), 32, 39, 46, 50 (b&w), 52 (b&w), 58 (b&w), 62 (b&w), 66 (b&w), 76 (b&w), 81 (b&w), 88 (b&w), 89 (b&w), 104, 116, 118 (b&w), 120 (b&w), 121 (b&w), 122 (b&w), 124, 136, 153 (b&w), 164, 166, 170, 176, 178, 180 (b&w), 190, 198, 203 (b&w), 204, 223, 229 (botttom right)
Iwan Baan: 225
Carolyn Doepke Bennett: 229 (top left)
Dryden Helgoe and Joe Sturges: 228
Doug Jamieson: 163
Marcia Lee: 2–3, 12, 35, 40–41, 43, 45, 50–52, 58 (top right), 59, 62, 66–69, 78–79, 85, 90–91, 94–95, 99–102, 105–7, 109, 110 (bottom right), 111 (top right), 120, 121, 155, 157, 158, 160–61, 165, 167–69, 171–73, 186–87, 194–95, 197, 199–201, 206, 210, 212, 216, 220–21, 225, 227, 229 (top right), 240
William Nicholas: 9
Victoria Pearson: 205, 209, 211, 213–15, 217–19
Tim Street-Porter: 7, 18, 21, 22 (color), 23, 24, 26 (color), 27–31, 55, 83, 84, 86–89, 92–93, 103, 108, 110, 111, 126–27, 129, 131, 193
Lisa Romerein: 5, 112, 113, 117–19, 122, 123, 125, 132, 133, 137–51, 159, 174, 175, 179–85
Joe Sturges: 15, 37, 57, 70, 75, 81, 97, 115, 130, 135, 153, 177, 189, 196, 203, 224, 226
Nat Zappia: 229 (bottom left)

All photographs © Nancy Goslee Power & Associates, Inc., except the following:
© Edmund Barr: 191
© Inner-City Arts: 228
© Nancy Goslee Power: 39, 46 (watercolors)
© Victoria Pearson: 1, 13, 33, 49, 53
© Tim Street-Porter: 34, 44, 47, 54, 58 (top left), 61, 63–65, 72, 73, 76, 77

Published in 2009 by Stewart, Tabori & Chang
An imprint of ABRAMS

Text copyright © 2009 Nancy Goslee Power

Library of Congress Cataloging-in-Publication Data
Power, Nancy Goslee.
    Power of gardens / Nancy Goslee Power; foreword by
        Bunny Williams.
        p. cm.
    Includes bibliographical references.
    ISBN 978-1-58479-757-9
    1. Gardens, American. 2. Gardens--Styles. 3. Gardens—Design. I.
Title.
    SB457.53.P69 2009
    712--dc22

                            2009018327

Editor: Jennifer Levesque
Designers: Doug Turshen with David Huang
Production Manager: Tina Cameron

The text of this book was composed in Bembo, Didot, and Requiem

Printed and bound in China
10 9 8 7 6 5 4 3 2 1

THE ART OF BOOKS SINCE 1949
115 West 18th Street
New York, NY 10011
www.abramsbooks.com